RELIGION AND MYTHOLOGY

Married of Necessity

Louis J. Hammann

University Press of America,® Inc.
Lanham • New York • Oxford

Copyright © 1998
University Press of America,® Inc.
4720 Boston Way
Lanham, Maryland 20706

12 Hid's Copse Rd.
Cummor Hill, Oxford OX2 9JJ

All rights reserved
Printed in the United States of America
British Library Cataloging in Publication Information Available

Library of Congress Cataloging-in-Publication Data

Hammann, Louis J.
Religion and mythology : married of necessity / Louis J. Hammann.
p. cm.
Includes bibliographical references.
l. Myth. 2. Religion. I. Title.
BL304.H36 1998 291.1'3—dc21 98-21041 CIP

ISBN 0-7618-1148-6 (cloth: alk. ppr.)
ISBN 0-7618-1149-4 (pbk: alk. ppr.)

∞™ The paper used in this publication meet the minimum
requirements of American National Standard for information
Sciences—Permanence of Paper for Printed Library Materials,
ANSI Z39.48—1984

For

Harry Buck
Scholar, Pilgrim, Friend

Sine quo non.

TABLE OF CONTENTS

ACKNOWLEDGMENT
PREFACE

PART I
RELIGION

CHAPTER I: SETTING THE STAGE FOR
UNDERSTANDING THE MARRIAGE OF
RELIGION AND MYTHOLOGY 1-11

CHAPTER II: HAS THE TIME COME TO
REDEFINE RELIGION? 13-32

PART II
MYTHOLOGY

CHAPTER I: MYTHMAKING AS A HABIT OF MIND:
FIRST CONSIDERATIONS 33-37

CHAPTER II: MYTHMAKING AS A HABIT OF MIND:
CIRCUMSPECTION 39-51

CHAPTER III: MYTHMAKING AS A HABIT OF MIND:
IMAGINING—HOW MYTHS ARE MADE .. 53-61

CHAPTER IV: MYTHMAKING AS A HABIT OF MIND:
FAMILIARITY—WHAT MAKES MYTHS
POSSIBLE (AND NECESSARY) 63-77

CHAPTER V: CODA TO PART II 79-82

PART III
*MYTHOLOGY IN THE
SERVICE OF RELIGION*

CHAPTER I: HISTORY IMAGINED AS TRUTH . 83-106

CHAPTER II: MYTHOLOGIES AS ALTERNATIVE
    VISIONS 107-128

CHAPTER III: SURROGATE MYTHS 129-140

CHAPTER IV: MYTHOLOGY AND RELIGION:
    PARTNERS IN A LANGUAGE GAME 141-147

Acknowledgments

Where do ideas come from and how do arguments develop? To me the stuff of this extended essay examplifies the mystery that shadows those two questions. Still, there are "the others"--a host of them--who have aided and abetted my personal cogitations. Without making any of them responsible for the faults of this undertaking, I must at least acknowledge them by name or class.

The students in my seminar at Gettysburg College have my appreciation for their patience and sometime confusion in trying to cope with these ideas and arguments.

Harry Buck (Professor Emeritus of Religion, Wilson College) has been my companion in this enterprise for longer than I dare remember. In fact, without his interest, sometimes parallel to mine and sometimes divergent, there would be no book in your hands. We have been together for a long time on the intellectual pilgrimage through the territory of Religion and Mythology.

Other colleagues have encouraged me and helped to straighten out my thoughts when they bent too far this way or that. Kerry Walters (Professor of Philosophy, Gettysburg College) was especially helpful at a certain critical stage of the journey--though he might not have realized it. And Steve Kennamer (*The Testimony of Peter Simons*) was a welcome counselor and critic also at a crucial stage of the work.

Kim Breighner (Computing Services, Gettysburg College) was more like a sculptor than a mechanic in shaping and repairing the manuscript.

My wife, Patricia, has been more than tolerant of my occasionally obsessive ways in trying to finish this task.

And the several audiences who actually heard me try to convey these ideas and arguments in a sensible language in finite time provoked me actually to say clearly what I thought. But no other person or class bears any responsibility for my confusion and mistakes than myself.

Finally I acknowledge the following for permission to use published materials:

John Seabrook for material from "Why Is The Force Still With Us?" in *The New Yorker,* January 6, 1997

"JFK: The Myth" by Andrew Kopkind, reprinted with permission
from the January 20, 1991 issue of *The Nation* magazine

Bantam Books for material from *Lila, An Inquiry into Morals*
by Robert M. Pirsig. Copyright, 1991

Bantam Books for material from *Emotional Intelligence:
Why It Can Matter More than IQ*
by Daniel Goleman. Copyright, 1995

A. Codrescu, *The Disappearance of the Outside* (pages 198, 200, 201)
© 1990 Andre Codrescu.
Reprinted by permission of Addison Wesley Longman.

From *Myths To Live By* by Joseph Campbell, Copyright © 1972
by Joseph Campbell. Used by permission
of Viking Penguin, a division of Penguin Putnam, Inc.

Orbis Books for material from *The Myth of Christian Uniqueness.*,
John Hick and Paul F. Knitter, editors. Copyright, 1992

Blackwell Ltd. for materials from *The Wittgenstein Reader*,
Anthony Kenny, editor. Copyright, 1995

PREFACE

I have often thought that religion and myth were one version of a primal couple, betrothed shortly after the first humans woke to find themselves in a world. The fundamentalist (i.e., quasi-scientific) version of religion, however, denies such an alliance. Myths, from that point of view, are contrivances of the human imagination and therefore falsehoods that mislead people. Hence they cannot be judged to bear any relationship with the revealed truth of a particular monotheism.

There are, of course, other ways to conceptualize both religion and myth that do not deny the possibility of a *bona fide* marriage between them. From the perspective that I shall try to find in these essays even fundamentalism may, paradoxically, be seen as a species of the genus "religion." Still, the quasi-scientific bias of fundamentalistic traditions would abrogate the alliance, since it appears to confuse revealed scripture with the falsehoods (that is, the myths) of pagan beliefs. The bias of the arguments that follow, however, does not recognize such a judgment. The problem that is unresolvable is that fundamentalistic traditions do not **understand** themselves in the way that historians of religion do. Even though that disagreement cannot be denied, it will not hold me captive as I try to **understand** the variety of religious traditions and the mythologies that form their substratum.

The following chapters, then, will seek to argue the claim that religion and myth, throughout the histories of culture, are in fact always married. In the course of time, the marriage may be compromised or attenuated. The stories (i.e., myths) that are foundational as well as ornamental may become detached and eventually secularized, that is, claimed by the culture as interpretive allusions and metaphors rather than conveyances of a superordinate truth. But "in the beginning" religion and myth were bound together as mutual surrogates.

As with any marriage (--we understand all too well in this part of the twentieth century--) the primeval romance may fade from consciousness and the parties may drift apart. Still, they are not likely to forget completely that one-time alliance in which mutuality redeemed both of them from loneliness. But we are talking here about exceptions. For in the "great traditions" the disposition to marry persists, even if the relationship eventually seems to be strained to the breaking point.

Here, perhaps, we should enter a cautionary note about the analogy. The notion of a "marriage" is only that, a notion, a figure of speech, a

Religion and Mythology

dramatic image, and I am interested in using it only so far as it helps us to get a hold of the complicated relationship of religion and myth.

I express this demur here in response to C. S. Kirk's judgment about the relation of myth and religion. In *Myth: Its Meaning And Function In Ancient and Other Cultures* Kirk responds to Cassier's assumption "that both [religion and myth] involve a passionate response to the world, that they are united by a special *intensity* of feeling."[1] Arguing that myths are not consistently or universally expressive of such "intensity," Kirk makes the following observation:

> ... Myths are not connected with religion any more by a universal emotional intensity than they are by their subject-matter--for, as has been seen, whereas some myths are about gods, others are not. *Therefore it will be wise to reject from the outset the idea that myth and religion are twin aspects of the same subject, or parallel manifestations of the same psychic condition, just as firmly as we rejected the idea that all myths are associated with rituals.*[2]

Granted that all myths are not about gods. On the other hand, neither is all religion "about gods." As I shall argue, mythic gods or God may provide a way of focusing the elemental experience of **relationships** that constitute religious experience. I shall also propose at the end of this discussion that mythmaking is such a persistent "habit of mind" that in fact it creates surrogate myths that are not necessarily wedded directly to religious experience. It is ironical, indeed, that "marriage," as a metaphor for the relation of myth and religion, should have the advantage of the reconfiguration of the institution of marriage in our own time. What was once, presumably, a thoroughly limited and often divinely sanctioned relationship between men and women seems to have become more ambiguous and less well-defined in our historical moment.

To speak of the marriage of religion and myth, allows for Kirk's cautionary note and still makes it possible to use the figure as an appropriate way of recognizing a relationship that is neither universal nor fixed in definition. In fact, the notion of a marriage avoids having to see religion and myth as "twin aspects of the same subject." Indeed,

Preface

marriages are always between parties whose differences are as conspicuous as their similarities. Religion and myth are, then, not "blood relatives," joined by an irresistible natural bond. They are not siblings, but only autonomous individuals that for mutual benefit and need enter into a useful contract. I ask the reader to keep this distinction in mind as I occasionally invoke the figure of marriage to specify the historically and psychologically complex relation of myth and religion.

There is, however, another analogy that drives this inquiry, though not at the level of argument. Imagine a playground at the local elementary school. But instead of children sliding, riding, swinging, and climbing, let the players be **ideas**. In scholarly inquiry we suppose that the mind controls its thoughts, moving them carefully and deliberately in a certain direction or maintaining a clear pattern of development. For many of us, however, thoughts and ideas seem more autonomous, enjoying a degree of freedom that our methodology may not be able to cope with. Hence, a reader must be prepared to watch those ideas sometimes at play in the field of the mind.

The Principal, of course, during his "appointed rounds," tries to exercise a degree of discipline on those under his supervision on the playground. In that capacity I shall try always to constrain these ideas that have for so long had their own way in my thoughts. Still, there may be times when the discipline seems to break down in face of overwhelming opportunities that arise as we attend to this occasional, though wondrous marriage of religion and myth. This is an alliance so old, so persistent, so elusive in how it manages itself that I confess ahead of time that I am more fascinated by it than sure that I understand it. Even though a good marriage is often a mystery even to the parties committed to it, we may learn something by observing it carefully. In what follows that is what I intend to do.

Notes

[1] (Berkeley and Los Angeles: University of California Press, 1970), p. 30.

[2] Kirk, p. 32 (emphasis mine).

PART I : RELIGION

CHAPTER 1

SETTING THE STAGE FOR UNDERSTANDING THE MARRIAGE OF RELIGION AND MYTHOLOGY

". . . sometimes I have believed as many as six impossible things before breakfast."
(The White Queen in *Alice in Wonderland*)

Attempts to understand both religious experience and mythmaking pose very difficult problems for philosophical reflection. Is it possible to conceive of these two persistent ways of responding to the world as constituting useful--or even valid--knowledge? Is it possible to understand "knowing" in such a way as to allow that religion and myth are not simply useless aberrations or benighted and desperate efforts to find some illusory consolation in a bewildering universe? On the other hand, is logical clarity or empirical reference the only features of thought that authenticate "truth claims"?

If we were to look for paragons of rationality in the Western tradition, we would surely find them not only in Immanuel Kant but also in Rodin's famous statue, "The Thinker." For Kant, "knowing" was a process played out by a mind already "programmed" with the *a priori* conditions that made "pure reason" possible. Rodin's statue, perhaps a bronze version of a Kantian philosopher, suggests a deliberate application of systematic thought to some particular problem to be solved or resolved. His (Its) determination is indicated by a fixed posture not to be compromised by distractions and by the wrinkled brow that signals a mind straining to walk a straight line to valid knowledge. Neither the philosopher Kant nor Rodin's Bronze give any hint that "knowing/thinking" is not necessarily confined to a willed application of the specialized protocols of rationality. Judging from these two icons, we have learned to live with the bias that *bona fide* knowledge is confined to what we know by "human reason"--as though reason, understood as a formal logical procedure, were the only operation that produces valid responses to the rush and variety of experience!

Some, of course, may practice that kind of intentional and logical enterprise to the near exclusion of other operations. But surely the human mind (better say "person") is capable of, or even inclined to, other modalities of thought and knowledge. The better the human brain is understood, the more varied seem to be its *modi operandi*. There is even now a book with the intriguing title, *Emotional Intelligence*.[1] Even before Goleman's popular exploration of "behavioral and brain sciences," Olive Sacks had tried to teach us to appreciate how idiosyncratic the mind can be. For him what may seem strange to ordinary humanity can still be found on the operational continuum of the "normal" mind.[2] There are also the artists whose creative abilities cannot easily be accounted for in theories of knowledge. Their particular way of "representing" experience so that it becomes accessible to the hearing and seeing of others seems to baffle such theories. So philosophers have avoided drawing art into the realm of epistemology by inventing aesthetic theory. But, surely, artists have minds and scientists have imaginations. Those who are badgered by their feelings are not necessarily devoid of logic.

If we remain captive to the epistemology that takes "reason" to be the only authentic arbiter of valid knowledge, then religion and myth along with art and much original science must be aberrations or at best anomalies in the human community. In order to broaden our appreciation of human knowing, we must learn to include a wider range of the operations than those indicated, quite uncertainly I might add, by the rubrics "reason" and "rational." How much more humane to encourage persons to "know" in whatever modality they find at hand!

Setting the Stage

Or did the Enlightenment so thoroughly skew our thinking that we can no longer grant validity to imagining and feeling, to intuition and envisioning? Must we foreswear any religious experience that cannot be recast as rational theology; must we denigrate myths that come to us as dramas rather than explanations? Unless we reconstruct epistemology along the lines of inclusiveness, we shall eventually dismiss an incredible range of *presumptive* knowledge. How ironic that some human minds would themselves indulge in such *presumption* merely to protect the appearance of "scientific" validity for knowledge claims.

For decades, many, if not most, Western scholars, with a penchant for the perspectives of social science, have theorized about religion and myth with virtually no charity to either.[3] Both are more often than not seen as mere curiosities that erupt out of the human enterprise or are taken as evidence that we have not yet lost our penchant for irrationality, that is, for "invoking immaterial beings and powers"[4] that many scholars disdain to "believe in." The unfortunate assumption seems to be that we may live long enough as a species to cure ourselves of these fantasies. Validity is so narrowly defined that the effusion of feeling and the flight of intuition, the imagining of the eye and the auditing of the ear, the evocations of the poet and the fabrications of the novelist, the instinct of the philosopher and the dreams of the mystic, the inventions of the scientist and the polemics of politicians--all such seem peripheral to reliable knowledge and beyond the range of traditional epistemology. This, despite the fact that through our history we have conjured and realized worlds in a stunning variety of ways! Unless we expand our epistemology to include, with appreciation, all such thought and knowledge, we may eventually feel obliged to reduce human culture to rational reflex and dogmatic construction.

So if my argument, the part that I have just begun to lay out and the part that still lies ahead, seems to be polemical, I have no apology. I would only protest that some provocation may be necessary to have us rearrange our assumptions about what constitutes knowledge. We have practiced the Enlightenment (and perhaps even the Aristotelian) habits of reflection so long now that we may not even realize what we lose when we take up residence in those cages. I trust, however, that one can be polemical (i.e., controversial) without being dismissive of

Religion and Mythology

what has been accomplished in the near endless sorting-out of how we know what we know. It would be paradoxical indeed if, in trying to caution against the kind of dismissiveness that religion and myth have been subjected to, I were to be dismissive of Kant and Rodin and that unnumbered host of philosophers (and now psychologists and social scientists) who have tried to conjure up rational (scientific?) explanations of what we do when we try to claim knowledge. If a new epistemology is not more generous than that, then it deserves little credibility in its own right.

But this is not the place to venture a complete reconstruction of epistemology in the Western tradition or to invoke *de novo* a unique theory of knowledge. My hope is more modest than that. I want only to find room in the domicile of human experience for religion and myth--and to celebrate their marriage. Human persons, in a vast variety of cultures, have displayed a cognitive repertoire that is, to say the least, impressive. I want only to appreciate--that is, to recognize the **value** for human survival--of such adaptability and ingenuity. I want simply to find room for what I will call "imagining" in the quest for knowledge and to claim some degree of legitimacy for that way of knowing. We may begin with an observation so obvious that it seems to have escaped the attention of many who have indulged in epistemological reflection.

There is a Greek verb "to know" (**oi'da** == *oida*) that is based on the perfect tense of the verb "to see" (**ei'dw** == *eido*). Hence "to know" is "to have seen"! Classical Greek, of course, has other verbs to indicate that most generalized process that we call "knowing." But one of the most recurrent and useful of that list preserves the intuitive realization that *knowing* and *seeing* are at least cousins in the familial repertoire of cognition.

With regard to the actual employment of our senses, we need only open our eyes to see, while hearing requires the more indirect procedure of "tuning in," paying attention, alerting our attention. In the human sensorium, then, seeing is, in some practical sense, primary. There is a moment that eludes our reflective understanding when we open our eyes and, without mustering our intentions, are able to discern, to "take in" what is there beyond our perceptual apparatus. The world, then, comes to us spontaneously as what is seen, that is, as an image so manifold in

Setting the Stage

content and complex in structure that the seer can hardly be aware of what has happened--or rather, what *is happening*--when she opens her eyes. Sight is imperious. It claims as much of the domain beyond our bodies as light falls upon. Even if one wants to assure another that she has understood a communication, she casually protests, "O, yes, I see," or even "I see what you mean." Buried in that easy response we may find an epistemological clue to the historical alliance of religion and myth.

One thing is clear about religions: They all have, somewhere near the foundations of their labyrinthine structures, stories that conjure real or imaginary events into dramatic portrayal. The relationship of religion and myth, then, is more than accidental. It is a marriage of primary experiences, a radical alliance of elemental dispositions. The offsprings of such a marriage may appear primarily as institutions; but the parents of such "churches," that is, religious experience and the impulse to mythmaking, are two ways of knowing that are reciprocal.

Mythical knowledge springs from that elemental moment of *seeing* the world. One need only open her eyes to see what is there, and what is there can only come to the seer directly. The world reproduces itself as image to our seeing. The seen, however, is not two or even three dimensional image. If we can think such a thought, our "imaginal" perception is at least four dimensional. The events that happen in space are spread through time as well. Myth, in significant part, is the dramatic rendition of nature reordered in historic or quasi-historic time.

Religions, dependent on, indeed rooted in such dramatic renditions, also *involve* the human observer in those imagined events. Ineluctably, of course, the myth is so familiarized in the course of its telling that religious folks cease making any critical distinction between what was and what is imagined. This marriage is consummated when a critical mass of individuals transmogrify into a community of "the faithful."

The thoughtful reflection of those who find themselves in such communities may eventually become "ambidextrous." That is, reflection within the enclave of the faithful "properly incorporates both analytical *and* imaginative processes."[5] The production of theologies and other rational reconstructions or justifications of the myth may manage to shake the foundations of a religious tradition, though it should not in the long run obliterate it. If a community ceases to "tell its story" or so thoroughly routinizes it, its *raison d'etre* may be compromised. Still, the story will not be lost to history, though it may survive only as an interesting historical residue. Many myths, of course, persist in metaphor and allusion, available to give current experience a dramatic resonance it might not otherwise have. The marriage of religion and myth may fade in memory and historical effect; it may imitate human marriage as its primal bonds of dependence erode under revolutionary--or evolutionary--changes in a culture. But the original "contract" is what we must try to discern.

For centuries religion has been defined as beliefs and those beliefs, it has been assumed, were best served by being translated into such propositional interpretations as creeds, metaphysical systems and theologies. If we suppose, however, that religion is primarily "imaginal experiencing," we might better appreciate the sheer persistence of the mythmaking habit and the incorporation of that habit into specific religious traditions.[6] Observing and appreciating that marriage of religion and myth--of religious experience and the habit of mythmaking--is the aim of these chapters.

It may seem presumptuous, indeed, to attempt the kind of binocular observation that "sees" myth and religion as having been intimately involved over the millennia. The efforts to define both of these phenomena separately have been enormous and intense. I shall argue, however, that they are best understood on analogy with partners in a marriage. It is the interdependency and reciprocity of these two responses to the world, these two modes of experience that illuminate religion and religions as well as myth and mythmaking. Both are attempts to turn the world into a familiar place by quite literally *imagining* that world, *experienced* in terms of *relationships.* In order to appreciate what happens when we try to see past the belief paradigm, we should be prepared to bring that very notion of "experience" under an epistemological umbrella that would protect it against the acid rain of purely rational criticism.

It is more likely than not that the philosophers and social scientists among us will fail to produce a definitive explanation of myth and religion taken separately. They, like the rest of us, are trapped in a strange dilemma: They would "explain" what they claim emerges into the human community as religion and myth by denying any real explanatory power to either of these persistent historical realities. But perhaps we need to abandon explaining, or at least to suspend our efforts to explain, those human creations that arise from impulses that are quite different from--or at least radical variations on--rational discourse and empirical observation. Neither religious experience nor mythmaking points to necessarily verifiable features or facts of the world. They have more to do with *comprehending* the objects of experience than with ex-plaining (that is, "flattening out") those objects of experience. It is more likely than not that the philosophers and social scientists among us will fail to produce a definitive explanation of myth and religion taken separately. They, like the rest of us, are trapped in a strange dilemma: They would "explain" what they claim emerges into the human community as religion and myth by denying any real explanatory power to either of these persistent historical realities. But perhaps we need to abandon explaining, or at least to suspend our efforts to explain, those human creations that arise from impulses that are quite different from--or at least radical variations on-- rational discourse and empirical observation. Neither religious experience nor mythmaking points to necessarily verifiable features or facts of the world. They have more to do with *comprehending* the objects of experience than with ex-plaining (that is, "flattening out") those objects of experience. After all, "explaining" is only one of many ways to comprehend what baffles or provokes the mind. Perhaps what we need is an epistemology that is more flexible or expansive than the classical dissection of "reason." Religious traditions avoid merely *explaining* the world or human experience by institutionalizing the effects of a community's commitment to a mythology. Mythmaking cooperates with religious experience, quite precisely, *i*by *imagining* the familiar. A religion, then, at least sponsors the drawing of pictures, celebrates the telling of stories and invites the faithful to converse in a myriad of ways. Both devotee and mythmaker *imagine* experience and thereby satisfy the subjective need to be in touch with an objective world by dramatizing it rather than explaining it.[7]

In appreciation of the White Queen's confession cited at the head of this Introduction, the next chapter will venture a "redefinition" of religion. Instead of thinking of religions as systems of *beliefs*, we shall venture to think of them as originating in, and sustaining *relationships* with, the objects of experience that confront human beings in the arenas of nature and history. I shall argue that beliefs are not the primary expression of religious experience. Rather, it is myths that dramatize the community-forming relationships that occur in those encounters with history and nature.

The chapters in Part II will try to explain the "habit of mind" that persists in making myths. They shall focus on the concepts of "familiarity" and "imagination" and the reciprocity of these two reflexes of the human mind and heart. The chapters in Part III will try to make sense of the actual employment of myth in religious traditions. Finally, as part of that undertaking I shall argue that the habit of mind that has made the "artifactual" myths that survive, at least as antique reminders of another world, continues to create "surrogate myths." This process persists in the present, where both historic and the unconventional religions are trying to work out a *modus vivendi* with a world they never made. Finally, I shall venture a coda that tries to appreciate the marriage of religion and myth.

I am still persuaded that religious experience and the mythmaking habit of mind need to find shelter in epistemology. However tempting it might be, I shall resist the task of refining a theory of knowledge that may spin off a blueprint of a domicile for the married couple. Eventually, perhaps, neurologists may enlist social scientists and historians to venture such a theory. Preoccupied as we are now with the revolution in communication technology and the Noah's flood of information, this kind of theoretical undertaking may have to wait. But sooner or later, some time short of the twenty-second century, we should respond to the challenge.

One may find at least a premonition of such a "unified field theory" in an idiosyncratic book by Leonard Shlain. In the last five chapters of *Art & Physics: Parallel Visions in Space, Time & Light* one may find the ground work of such a theory that tries to comprehend the full range of our mental operations.[8] The author is himself a surgeon and not a philosopher, though he "boldly goes where no one has gone before." There at the edge of the galaxy of conventional ideas, he quotes Rudy Rucker: "I am, as it were, an eye that the cosmos uses to look at itself. The Mind is not alone; the Mind is everywhere." If some were actually to wake up to the prospect that "the Mind is everywhere" and is, in

Setting the Stage

some sense "an eye that the cosmos uses to look at itself," we may discover a perspective from which religion and myth constitute authentic knowledge. In that search we may discover a primeval marriage that imitates the mythical union of Earth and Sky from which all thing arise and in which is resolved that most elemental human impulse to convert the chaos of the world into the cosmos of experience.

Notes

1 Daniel Goleman, *Emotional Intelligence: Why It Can Matter More Than IQ* (New York: Bantam Books, 1995). Goleman's book is in no way a contribution to a "new epistemology." His interests are "psychological" rather than "philosophical." His focus on the varieties of "intelligence" does not lead him to search for the empirical basis of **knowledge**. His book is more interested in "a different way of being smart" and hence in how to operate in "real life," rather than solving the persistent philosophical problems of how to determine what is true or what is valid knowledge. Still, in our effort to determine what we know when we have created myths by *imagining* the full range of possible experiences, any clue to how the human person "knows" what she "knows" should be held in our attention. But, to be clear: I cite this book only as an example of the sheer complexity--and consequent ambiguity--of what I would call *bona fide* knowledge. Still, there is a passage that provides some insight into mythmaking: "Some of us are naturally more attuned to the emotional mind's special symbolic modes: metaphor and simile, along with poetry, song, and fable, are all cast in the language of the heart. So are dreams and myths, in which loose associations determine the flow of narrative, abiding by the logic of the emotional mind." (p. 54)

2 See, for example: *The Man Who Mistook His Wife for a Hat* (New York: Perennial Library, 1987); *Anthropologist on Mars: Seven Paradoxical Tales* (New York: Knopf, 1995); and *Awakenings* (New York: Harper Perennial, 1990.).

3 In a recent issue of the *Bulletin / CSSR* (Volume 24,, Number 3,4) Russell McCutcheon surveyed the scholarship focused on "methodology and theory" in the study of religion. He notes that the International

Religion and Mythology

Association of History of Religion is committed "to conceptualizing religion as a historical phenomenon, to engage in empirically-based research, all of which is part of the larger project of studying human culture. Such a strong historically-based declaration flies in the face of alternative conceptions of the field that are notoriously vague, ill-defined, ahistorical, and speculative, all of which contributes to the general identity crisis which has traditionally characterized the study of religion." (p. 57)

For further insight into the current study of religion, see J. Samuel Preus, *Explaining Religion: Criticism and Theory from Bodin to Freud* (Yale University Press, 1987); Hans H. Penner, *Impasse and Resolution: A Critique of the Study of Religion* in the Toronto Studies in Religion series (Peter Lang, 1989); Benson Saler *Conceptualizing Religion: Immanent Anthropologists, Transcendent Natives, and Unbounded Categories* (E.J. Brill, 1993); and Daniel L. Pals, *Seven Theories of Religion* (Oxford University Press, 1996). The first and third of these studies are concerned with the study of religion in historical perspective. Penner's book, on the other hand aims at making a positive contribution to "the resolution" of the dilemmas that haunt the study of religion.

For still other contributions to critical scholarship, see McCutcheon's article, *passim* and in Saler "References Cited."

4 McCutcheon, *Bulletin /CSSR*, p. 59.

5 Kerry S. Walters, "Critical Thinking, Logicism, and the Eclipse of Imagining," in *The Journal of Creative Behavior*, Volume 26, no. 2, Second Quarter, 1992; p. 142, *et passim*. Emphasis mine.

6 For an explanation of this ingenious distinction, see Kerry S. Walters, p. 140 *et passim*.

7 An original elaboration of this notion can be found in Stewart Guthrie's *Faces in the Clouds: A New Theory of Religion* (New York and Oxford: Oxford University Press, 1993). In support of the claim that "religion *is* anthropomorphism," Guthrie summarizes his argument as follows: ". . . [T]he progenitors of religions are our perceptual uncertainty and our need to see any people who are present. Religions are a family in that all are born from the search for human form and behavior, and all constitute claims to have found such form and behavior in the nonhuman world. However, their ancestry results in a more positive unity than mere family

resemblance. All religions do share a feature: ostensible communication with humanlike, yet nonhuman, being through some form of symbolic action." (p. 197)

8 Leonard Shlain, *Art & Physics: Parallel Visions in Space, Time & Light* (New York: William Morrow, 1991), especially chapters 25 through 29.

CHAPTER II

HAS THE TIME COME TO REDEFINE RELIGION?

> "We believe what we want to believe."
> (Anonymous)

If we are going to observe closely the marriage of myth and religion, we ought to be sure that we agree on the identity of the two parties. In Part II, I shall raise certain questions about mythmaking: what is the precondition of this "habit of mind" and how does it play itself out? In this chapter, I shall raise--and try to answer--the single question of the title.

I shall argue that the answer to that impertinent question is, yes. But first let me put down the footings if not the foundation of the project. In a remarkable work that tried to marry philosophical and anthropological insights, Rodney Needham concluded that:

> In one respect or another, therefore, the words in which we cast our thoughts and communications may not always have the usefulness that we are inclined to ascribe to them. We can only rely upon them, yet often, and perhaps even characteristically, they are unreliable. They lead us to imagine that we can say what we think, and conversely that we think what we say; but neither of these inferences is necessarily correct, and in the case of *belief* they are both false.[1]

Further on, Needham quotes MacIntyre to the effect that "[Behaviorists] may have underrated the extent to which we are very often opaque to each other a great deal of the time. *Misunderstanding and not understanding [is] at the core of human life.* . . ."[2] Often what appears to be conversations among human beings is more like the whistles that we blow even as we rush through the landscape of a common culture in trains passing in the night. Just as a poem, for Robert Frost, may be a temporary stay against confusion, so beliefs may be also, especially amid what Needham calls "the phantasmagoric variegation of the collective forms of significance."

In an effort to evoke an appreciation of such authentic confusion, Needham invokes a familiar conundrum from one of the twentieth century's most famous physicists:

> Einstein once remarked that 'the eternally incomprehensible fact about the universe is that it is comprehensible.' The solitary comprehensible fact about human experience is that it is incomprehensible.[3]

The observation is not only cogent by virtue of its strange symmetry but because it resonates with ordinary intuition. Making absolutistic claims for the validity or salvific potency of religious beliefs is counterintuitive. If we can, in discourse about religion as well as in the myriad efforts to give expression to religious experience, find a surer way to express ourselves than in the reflexive invocation of beliefs, we may find ourselves in trains that do not pass each other in the night at break-neck speeds. It is the direction and intention of this essay to slow us down and to modulate the whistles that we blow at each other in our passage through the nighttime landscape of the culture. Where shall we begin?

It is tempting first of all to look for some culprit that has skewed our understanding of religion or of religious traditions in the direction of "beliefs." The easiest to single out, of course, are those very religious traditions that are held captive by their own absolutistic bias. These are the "revealed religions" that justify their "faith and practice" by referring them to a single source that, presumably, intruded into human history at its own will to "uncover" (i.e., "to re-veil") the truth about this world and its creative author. Since such truth establishes itself as the "will of God," it brooks no compromise, no alternative, no ambiguity. Once those who own it have sufficient political power, they may then define the truth for any and all who fall under their influence. The social instruments of such power are formulas of belief that defend establishments against heresies or heterodoxies. These beliefs eventually consolidate themselves as orthodoxies that create a high degree of communal conformity. Quasi-political institutions, founded on such formulas, eventually become powerful enough to transform language, thought and feeling into imperious ideologies. "Followers" are then trapped in a strange paradox: They feel obliged to *believe* that only **others** are captives of a relativism that disqualifies their truth claims.

There are, however, signs that some Christians, for example, are trying to find their way out of this kind of trap. They are trying to extricate themselves from an absolutistic bias that not only deprecates the religious experience and convictions of others but may even condemn them to "the outer darkness." Since Christian imperialism has been so conspicuous over so many centuries, it is fascinating (and encouraging) to read the essays in a book entitled, *The Myth of Christian Uniqueness*. In the Preface one finds a necessary confession:

> Christianity, of course, is unique in the precise and literal sense in which every religious tradition is unique--namely that there is only one of it and that there is therefore nothing else exactly like it. But in much of Christian discourse, "the uniqueness of Christianity" has taken on a larger mythological meaning. It has come to signify the unique definitiveness, absoluteness, normativeness, superiority of Christianity in comparison with other religions of the world.[4]

In an act of creative courage, Gordon Kaufman, in the first essay in this volume, seeks a way out of or through such a conventional version of the Christian tradition: "In the past we could ask, What are the principal doctrines or ideas prescribed by tradition for Christians *to believe*, and how should we interpret them today?"[5] He then shifts the reader's attention to a quite different perspective:

> It now becomes necessary to direct attention to questions like, How does one articulate a worldview--specifically the Christian worldview--and how does one assess its significance for human life today? Refocusing religious reflection in this way leads one to attend to a rather different agenda from that followed by most theologians in the past. Instead of concentrating on familiar doctrines and dogmas, one is led to inquire into the fundamental categories--the basic conceptual and symbolic framework--that

Religion and Mythology

has given Christian perspectives their unique structure, order, and experiential flavor.[6]

The entire vocabulary associated with defining and declaring *beliefs* is being displaced, here, by such notions as "worldview," "reflection," "framework," "perspectives," and "experiential." Clearly, the rhetoric of a distinctive Christian discourse and the claims usually embedded in it are here undergoing a significant sea-change. But how shall we understand religion without the traditional reliance on the rhetoric of *belief* and *believing* ? This essay proposes a way out of this seeming impasse. Rather than define religion or religious experience in those well-established terms, I shall propose that we can single out a universal aspect of human experience that is prior to, more elemental and intuitively obvious than "religious beliefs."

Kaufman himself may give us an angle from which to approach this problem. In an effort to build a bridge between Christian theology and "other religious activity and reflection," he observes that even the former may understand itself "... as human imaginative response to the necessity to find orientation for life in a particular historical situation."[7] This does not commit Kaufman to finding some kind of a universal "spirituality" on which the Christian tradition is merely a special variation. I shall argue, however, even beyond Kaufman's reflections, that the option available is more intuitively persuasive than a popular reference to "spirituality." But one thing, so far, is clear: For some at least, the *kairos* for redefinition has come. The time is ripe for a concerted intellectual effort to redefine religion.

A couple of years ago, flying into Seattle on a night flight, we looked out the window and saw Mount Rainier, cloudless and bathed in the light of the full moon directly overhead. A stunning sight! Later in the week, we drove out to the mountain and up the slope as high as a car can go, about 6000 feet from the summit. An awesome sight! Still later we drove down to the remnants of Mount Saint Helen. As my grandmother used to say, "A sight to behold!" Then we visited the IMAX theater in Seattle and saw the film depicting the eruption of the volcano. By that time I was ready to dream about mountains.

And that is what happened. But it was a strange dream, indeed; a dream of absolute frustration. I dreamt that I was trying to repair

Has the Time Come to Redefine Religion?

Mount Saint Helen! To rebuild it, to restore it! I don't remember how I was trying to do it; I remember only the sense of helpless frustration that kept me from sleeping, while it couldn't quite wake me up. I was caught somewhere east of the great Dreaming.

That dream came to mind as I tried to get a hold of my thoughts about religious discourse, the kind that describes "religions," the kind that presumes to understand "religion" and the kind that tries to conjure with religious experience. And I began to compare the enormity--and seeming uselessness--of trying to repair Mount Saint Helen to the task that I allude to in the title of this chapter: Redefining religion. At some moment in my intellectual pilgrimage I realized that I was committed to trying to repair the shattered volcano, that is, to redefining religion. For a while the tasks seemed equally hopeless. But my intuition convinces me that the time **has** come--at least for some of us--to take up this enormous and **presumptuous** task.

I worry, of course, that my title may be so confusing that some may respond with a shrug of the shoulders--and drift off to explore other worlds. I can only hope that I am addressing persons for whom shrugging off any intellectual or affective challenge is not a likely response. So, here and now, I give up worrying about anyone dismissing the question that I began with: "Has the time come to redefine religion?" As I have indicated above, my answer is, yes; but, still, I should make **some** effort to justify the question and, eventually, to clarify the answer.

But first let me tell a story that may put this effort into perspective. A couple of years ago during a sleepless night in Managua, Nicaragua, I was staring at a wall map of the country and the region. I was faintly aware of music and distant agitation outside. It was the year in which Nicaraguans would celebrate (or lament!) what some called "The Triumph" and others "the disaster." I had been in Nicaragua about two weeks and was already overwhelmed by the environment of this "third world country." The pervasive dilapidation, the obvious poverty, the political tension in the air--all conspired to force upon me a glaring paradox: The only thing worse than no revolution is a revolution; the only thing worse than a revolution is no revolution.

I have been haunted by that thought ever since, even when I think of something as abstract as the "industrial revolution"--which recently

Religion and Mythology

provoked many of us to reflect on the bizarre logic of the "unabomber." Of course, there are also the many political turn-arounds and turn-overs of our long history, and especially of this century. Now reshaping our immediate world is the "information revolution" and its companion, the "communications revolution." It is easy to be overwhelmed by these modern blessings. But whenever I get nostalgic about the pre-whatever revolutionary days, my mind also conjures up a favorite myth: King Canute, the legendary character who stood in the English channel to beat back the ocean tides with a rope. He should have known that "time and tide wait for no one." Change--whether slow or sudden, benign or violent--is indigenous to the human situation. History is a great revolving--if not always a *bona fide* revolution.

It may be that some folks are at least occasionally wary, maybe weary, of the traffic on the information superhighway that is the latest phase of the "industrial revolution." Others may feel lost or at least apprehensive when they wander into the Worldwide Web or launch small boats on the Internet. Washing at the walls of these labyrinths one hears--or feels--the sensual and addictive march of images parading as knowledge that infiltrates our minds by way of television and the movies. (Need I give examples?) Meanwhile, all the other more antiquated carriers of information continue to tag along, and any of us may be tempted to say to this relentless barrage, this restless river of sound and silence and sight, "Enough!" Why can't I be happy with what is, rather than continue to lust for the "new whatever" that barrels down the cultural highway at break-neck speed? Enough already! The world is changing too fast. Alas! Should we join King Canute as he swings his flimsy rope against the relentless tide?

I am tempted to join the King, but cannot and will not, even to defend that venerable notion, that rubric, that ghost of our fading past, "religion." That is, I am going to try to repair Mount Saint Helen. Some will want to say about the mountain and about religion, "Is nothing sacred"? Surely something as deeply rooted in history and in the human psyche as religion is can be left alone. Why even suggest that we change our definition, our understanding of that ancient, maybe even eternal, fact of life? Is not "religion" at least an available refuge from the whirl that the world has become? At least leave religion alone or what goes next?

Has the Time Come to Redefine Religion?

First of all, the thought of **defining** religion at all may seem useless. Each of us probably has some personal notion that seems sufficient to our own use, so why undertake a public discussion about such a private matter? Isn't religion a strictly personal experience--and, to make matters worse, who can "define" an experience anyhow? There is surely no more elusive notion (or word) in the English language than that. Except, perhaps, "religion"! But "where" does that happen? Inside of my mind (or heart!) or out there in some social or political arena? Is religion only and exclusively an internal, strictly personal experience? Or is there something "out there" that corresponds to that notion that we invoke so casually?

Here is the dilemma: As soon as people begin to discuss religion as though it were something "out there," most of us find ourselves retreating into our private space, unwilling to test our own understanding and shy about challenging others who seem quite sure of their own experience. That does not mean that I or others carry around in our heads even a working definition of religion. It is, after all, an **experience** --and who would venture to figure out what an experience is? The range of references that word has is staggering.

Think how many moments, fleeting or sustained, critical or casual; how many glimmers of hope or apparitions of fear; how many flutters of the ego or intrusions of another presence that simple word "experience" applies to! **What** we experience as human beings and how we experience anything is a virtual mystery. After all, what really goes into an "experience" and how does it happen? Add the adjectives "personal" or "private" to the noun "experience" and you have the most baffling thought imaginable.

If religion is such a personal experience, who would venture to define such a thing, to set limits to such a notion? Now a perfect stranger comes along and asks, "Has the time come to re-define religion?" Can this be a serious undertaking: Re-define what we cannot or would rather not define in the first place? So, shall we drop the matter; or perhaps turn to hunting for wild mushrooms or snipes in the forests of our imaginations.

The question, however, will not evaporate so easily. In my judgment the question is critical, urgent, timely. On the other hand, I do not hope to change the world significantly by raising the question or

Religion and Mythology

risking an answer. Most people will go on for the next ten or fifty or a hundred years, unscathed by the questions I want to raise in this discussion. Still, the effort may help some folks bring their own elusive experience into focus. Perhaps some may see their own experience in relation to several thousand years of history and be able to clarify that aspect of experience that they may casually describe as "religious."

Still, is there any reason to risk getting lost in pursuit of such an elusive goal? Why redefine what most people would rather not define in the first place? After all, "religion" is not just a word in the dictionary. It is not even a "something" that asks to be "defined." It is an experience, and we can be sure that any attempt to define experience may feel like a wet blanket thrown over the coals of a personal fire in the heart. But the pursuit of such a goal need not turn one into a spoil sport. I think we might actually enjoy religion if we had some historical perspective on what it is--or at least on what we have come to think it is.

Here I am going to argue that it is not **only** what we have come to think it is. It was something different and, in fact, may still be something different from what we have come to think it is.

Where shall we start? It is a hazard to sensible inquiry merely to refer, at such moments as this, to a dictionary definition of words or terms. For the moment, however, we may want to suspend the protocols of specialized research and resort to the *American Heritage Dictionary* as an opener: *Religion:* "The expression of man's belief in and reverence for a superhuman power recognized as the creator and governor of the universe." This particular definition is not at all exceptional. First of all, it refers to "a power," as though polytheistic traditions were not religions. More telling, however, most, and perhaps all, dictionary definitions of religion include the notion of "belief" especially "in a superhuman or supernatural power." It is precisely that notion that I want to challenge.

But these are notions so deeply embedded in ordinary religious discourse that raising doubts about their validity or accuracy may only cause confusion and resistance. In a speech delivered just a couple of years ago, William Barr, who was then Attorney General of the U.S., was making the claim that "those committed to the Judeo-Christian

Has the Time Come to Redefine Religion?

values have made our country great." In support of that rhetorical claim, he offered a quick historical judgment: ". . . the Europeans did bring something that was new [to this continent]. They brought a *set of beliefs*--the Judeo-Christian tradition--a moral culture which provided a critique of injustice and a compelling account of man's true dignity."[8] So, by conventional definition, the Judeo-Christian tradition consists of a "set of beliefs." If that is what the tradition **seems to have become** over the centuries of its being secularized and politicized, is that what it was or is experientially? Was that tradition, at its beginning, a "set of beliefs"? Or is that all it is even now, after all those years of being tamed by European emperors and American culture, by philosophers and anthropologists?

In a well known and very long PBS series, Bill Moyers interviewed Joseph Campbell to find out what he thought about mythology. Shortly into the second interview, Moyers was trying to figure out what impact the culture of science has had on religion, and he came up with the following observation: "Science has made a housecleaning of [our religious] beliefs." Again, religion is wedded to beliefs. In competition with scientific method and the scientific worldview, how do religious beliefs fare in that game? Moyers' domestic metaphor suggests that maybe science has swept the Western religious establishment clean. Beliefs have been swept away--and therefore, religion has been swept away? Well, if religious experience is primarily or exclusively confined to statements of belief, then science wins the day with its experiments and its theories. Yes, but only if we insist on this equation of religious experience with belief.

The understanding of religion as "belief in" a superhuman force or person or presence has a history, of course. This is the definition that presents religion as, in a fundamental sense, a creed, a formula of beliefs that qualify one for "belonging to" some community of the faithful. But I want to argue that religious experience has not always been understood as the acceptance of a creed, has not always been limited to assertions of belief. For, that after all, is what *credo* meant: to believe this instead of that, "X" instead of "Y." But what does believing have to do with anything? What does believing have to do with what or how or why the universe is what it is--or seems to be? What does believing have to do with what I am or why I am what I am?

Religion and Mythology

Surely Anonymous was correct when he said, "We can believe what we want to believe!"

Let me be blunt: Does believing something have anything to do with the truth, validity or power of what beliefs affirm? To put the matter in colloquial terms: Does believing make anything so? If I believe in god, does that mean that god has to exist, or is religion, as that old conundrum insisted, "believing the unbelievable"? But why would anyone want to believe what was unbelievable--especially when there are so many believable things to believe? By that definition is being religious simply a way of playing a joke on ourselves? of fooling ourselves? of providing some false hope in face of a gnawing despair? Is being religious only a way of consoling ourselves in face of our suspicion that life is a tale told by an idiot, full of sound and fury, signifying nothing? Is religious experience simply a charade that plays out on the stage of our own minds? Is it no more than a self-generated entertainment to distract ourselves from facing an empty or chaotic universe; to keep ourselves sheltered against the hurricanes that blow through history; to keep ourselves from feeling the insanity that ripples through ordinary life?

Now, some may want to make the distinction between "believing in" and "believing that." But even though the historic creeds of Christendom are translated, "I believe **in** God," as though we were simply expressing a trust in a supreme being and not exactly making the proposition that God exists, the effect of the creeds has always been an assertion of a distinct and definitive existence and not only an expression of subjective confidence. "To believe in" is tantamount "to believing that" the god one believes in actually exists out there, fulfilling our hopes and allaying our fears, and executing promises of safety and prosperity. So to affirm **a belief in** god is somehow tangled up with a conviction and implies an assertion that there really **is** a god to "believe in."

But all of those puzzles aside: The historical Christian tradition (usually understood as "the Christian Church") has, over the centuries effectively defined religious experience in terms of "**believing** X to be true," as though X had to be true or one shouldn't or wouldn't "believe" it. Against this historical habit of mind I want to propose a quite different way of understanding religion.

Has the Time Come to Redefine Religion?

Again I want to break the protocols of argument and turn to a dictionary, this time not to the definition but to the etymology. It is quite usual for "religion" to be traced to two Latin words: one is the prefix *re-* which means something like "back or again" (as in "re-turn"); the other, and more important root, is *ligare*--a Latin verb that has provided many words to English: Col**le**ge, colle**a**gue; li**ga**ment, **liga**ture, **liga**tion; al**ly**, **lien**, ob**lige** and the like. But what do all these words and terms have in common? "Colleagues" are people bound together by some common commitment or obligation; a "college" is a collection of "colleagues." "Ligament" is a good derivative that will get us close to what I want to argue: A "ligament" ties or binds two things together. And "allies" are people bound together in a common cause. Some may remember that old Christian hymn, "Blessed be the tie that binds...." It all adds up to this: Whatever else we "believe," we harbor a suspicion that religious experience is **the sense of being tied to something,** though at this point I am reluctant to identify just what it is we may be tied to.

First I want to enlarge and generalize the notion that is embedded in the verb "to tie," *ligare*. Long before human beings are moved to formulate beliefs in their efforts to "define" themselves, I want to argue, there is a fundamental **experience** that is well-neigh universal. What really defines human beings are the relationships that tie us to--What?

With this question, I am beginning to run against the stream of conventional ways of understanding "religion." Let me illustrate what I mean by "conventional," by the sort of casual, common sense notions of what being religious means. On the cover of a flyer put out by a protestant denomination I found an interesting juxtaposition. Under the name of the denomination one reads: "Who we are. What we believe." So many Christians, and other religious folks as well, gain some part of their identity by what they believe and what they believe determines what they belong to. In denominational Christianity, believing X and Y and Z is a condition for belonging to a particular group or community. Formulas of belief--creeds--are like pledges of allegiance that tie one to particular institutions. And such belonging certainly contributes to who one is as well as what one is. Our sense of identity usually is shaped in part at least by connections and affiliations, that is, by what we belong to. But is the notion of religious experience exhausted by the notion of belonging to a particular community of belief? Is that what religion is exclusively or originally? Not according to my argument. It may have come to be defined in terms of belief and belonging. But my intuition and the evidence tell me that this is not an adequate definition of religion.

I hope I am not completely alone in seeking to reclaim religious experience as something prior to, as something over and above belonging to a particular community of people who have chosen to believe X, Y and Z, and, thereby, have chosen not to believe A, B and C. Still, I cannot shake off the sense that such affiliations, however practical and functional they may be, do not really satisfy our need for a more comprehensive relationship with what we might glibly call "the world" and all that may suggest.

In an elemental sense religious experience relates us to reality; it holds out the possibility of some connection with what is true, perhaps with what is real. In fact, choosing to believe "this or that" may waylay or mislead our energies. Choosing to believe certain answers to the big questions, religious folks provide themselves a kind of stopgap, a kind of consolation, a kind of therapy against worry and uncertainty. Even if such decisions allow us "to get on with life," they also narrow the range and depth of the elemental **relationships** that define us as denizens of the universe.

So, choosing to believe X, Y and Z, in significant part, establishes a formal relationship with an institution or community. It's like a pledge of allegiance. Such institutions tend to insist that "belonging" is a significant part of the definition of who one is, but surely there is more to being human than affiliation. Besides, despite what we tell ourselves, believing does not make anything so. Too often our quest for truth ends just inside the gate of belief.[9] And if beliefs are simply choices that we make, the quest for identity and connection ends even before it begins.

It comes down to this: When formulas of belief connect us with some historical community, too often that is enough; that is what being religious means. But what about the larger relationships, the elemental connections; what about the ecstatic participation in the drama of things? What about our relationships with the titanic forces of nature, with the whispering wind and the roaring rivers and gigantic

Has the Time Come to Redefine Religion?

mountains? What about our alliances with the authentic heroes of our imaginations? What about our affinities with other souls and spirits that haunt either our minds or the world itself? What about our relationships with what we remember and with what we have forgotten? It is not by mere **beliefs** that we are connected to the cosmos and to history. Relationships can thrive without their being married to beliefs--which are, I would allege, choices. But such choices may limit our feelings, confine our imaginations, encircle our thoughts.

Perhaps we choose certain beliefs not because they confirm the truth of things, but because they provide an antidote to the elixir of wonder and ambiguity and mystery. If who I am is determined only by what I believe, then my universe collapses in on itself and I have gained only the comfort of a fragile certainty. I may know what I believe, but I may thereby have built a wall around my heart and mind. Such a wall serves both to protect me from others whose beliefs are different from mine and, at the same time, excludes others from my universe. Every wall has two sides.

Let me make sure I have made myself clear: The fundamental religious experience, the psychological or personal or communal moment that comes long before we begin to say what we **believe** and therefore what we **deny** or choose not to believe--that moment in our personal history is a relationship or relationships. Let me be specific.

The "religion" of the Oglala Sioux depends on--is an expression of--their relationship with the Black Hills in what we now call Dakota. The followers of the Buddha were held together and their lives shaped by a relationship with Siddartha Gotama, both before and after he died. The religion of the Australian Aborigines is rooted in their sense that there is an "alternative universe" continuous with the one they inhabit and to which they have intimate ties through the mediation of shamans and dreams. This parallel universe is called "the Dreaming." That is where the ancestors live and other spirits, benign and hostile. But what sense would it make to say that Aborigines "believe in" the Dreaming? Rather, they live on the borderland of the Dreaming and, it seems, know occasionally how to enter it.

In one of the many supplementary reports that came along with the Pope's most recent visit to the U.S. (in 1995), a journalist visited a monastery in New Jersey. When quizzed about what he had to give up to belong to that particular order, the monk shifted the conversation to what he called "a relationship with the mysterious Jesus." A nun in another place talked about "keeping a line open to God." These unconventional practitioners of "the faith" had some sense that "belonging to the church" was not the central experience that kept them going in their religious vocations. This seems to be true, no matter how one responds to their piety.

Religious experience is as much a matter of being **unable** to imagine that there is no Dreaming or that the Black Hills are not sacred or that the Buddha was just a frustrated prince of northern India. The monks and nuns were **unable** to imagine a universe absent a suffering savior or a God ensconced in a cosmic telephone switch board. We could walk our way through the varieties of human religious experience and find at their bottom, rooted in their earliest historical moments, relationships that were felt so deeply that the only sensible response to the experience was to tell a story about it. It is the mythmaker who translates such experiences into dramatic tales that sustain both an individual and a communal sense of identity.

I am talking about relationships with places in the natural universe or with historical moments or with remembered persons. I am talking about relationships with a world or with a land or with a family. Relationships with seascapes or with an inner landscape, with the sun and the wind; with one's grandparents and one's children; relationships with forgotten memories and unfulfilled hopes; relationships with a house or a game, with a pain or with a fleeting joy. The possibilities and actualities are legion, numberless, and beyond our explaining. Surely, many of us find ourselves drawn into experiences that do not need to be explained but only celebrated; that do not need to be proven but only remembered. These experiences are the raw material out of which myths are imagined.

These foci of experience constitute what I would call the "foreground relationships" that simultaneously reveal and conceal the Other that envelopes our consciousness, that looms as the mystery that overwhelms perception, that baffles our ordinary faculties. Behind the foreground and beyond, is the chaos that is continuous with cosmos. The imagination may conjure a family of gods to preside over that other world that intersects this one. The mind may struggle to tame that

Has the Time Come to Redefine Religion?

Other with the harness of reason or with an attribution of reality. The heart may long to imitate its song, to conjure its appearance, to see and hear beyond the foreground that conceals it in an ecstasy of dark shadows or blinding light, or to revel in it as drama in which stage and audience change places.

Such foreground relationships are myriad and specific, reflections of time and place, shaped by perspective and expectation. They are the immediate foci of a relationship that confronts and affronts, that surrounds and subverts, a relationship that may be at the same time inclusive and exclusive. How many myths and visions and thoughts have we employed to tell ourselves and each other what such a relationship is and what it is not? But always the foreground is a glass, however dark, through which we see--or believe we see--into the deep shallows of reality where the human person may not be able to distinguish self and other, this and that, the fullness and the emptiness, chaos and cosmos.

The argument is this: Religion or religious experience is not something external to our fundamental experience; it is not exceptional, in the sense that it is confined only to what is superhuman or supernatural. It is **not** outside of the human order of things. It may itself be mysterious; it may be responsive to a mystery. It is not, however, in itself supernatural nor need we suppose that it is a response to the supernatural, requiring one to **believe** this or that. I doubt that the earliest Christians had any reason to believe **that** Jesus was the Messiah. Those who were allied to him early on were drawn into a relationship, in the foreground of consciousness, that must have been a strange combination of hope and fear, of historical memories and threatened ethnic identity. They were surrounded by a foreign army of occupation while they were haunted by ancestral memories of Abraham and Moses and David. Theirs must have been a fearful and inspiring relationship with a rabbi whose words were almost familiar and whose deeds were often confusing.

But the same kind of foreground scenario could be reconstructed for those encouraged by Confucius or Muhammad or Crazy Horse or Zoroaster. For those who found themselves living in the presence of Mount Olympus or Mount Meru, of Fujiyama or Mount Rainier, of the Matterhorn or Everest. For those who were intimate with the Nile

Religion and Mythology

or the Mississippi, with the Amazon or the Tiber, with the Rhine or the St Lawrence, with the Tigris and Euphrates or the Ganges. For those haunted by the tales of the invisible beings whose power manifests itself in the earth's fertility or in the hurricane or in the typhoon or in the burning sands of the great deserts; or in the rainforests of central America or in the cedar forests of Lebanon or in the Redwood groves of northern California.

I am talking about any and every relationship that **binds** a person or his kin or his larger community to the moments that overpower memory, to the silent and invisible presences that inspire our consciousness and haunt our unconscious; to connections real and imagined; to affinities felt and denied; to death anticipated and life immediately felt; to relationships that we cannot define but that define ourselves. I am talking about the foreground relationship that is opaque--or transparent--to a vision that conjures the universe into being as a place where humans can live without being threatened by its emptiness or its fullness, by its glowing invisibility or by its dark appearance.

But in this redefinition, what about God or the gods? I am arguing that religion is the celebration of fundamental **foreground relationships** that are continuous with a reality that spreads outward and inward in a simultaneous fugue of hope and fear. Eventually the relationships give way to formulas of belief that displace the original experience. When this happens, then God is no more and no less than one of the ways the all-encompassing, the overwhelming relationship with the ultimate "background" is brought into and held in focus by our ordinary consciousness. God is the face or the presence that haunts the Black Hills, the Nile or the invisible array of our ancestors. Divinity is the aura surrounding an historic personality in whom great historical processes converge. God is the name given to some felt presence that washes through our perceptions, our fears, our exaltations. For some that aura is so clear, that silence so resounding, that face so compelling that the human imagination conjures a being with its own life and its own power. A presence, often so human-like that it seems more than human, springs into life with such vividness that some cannot deny its reality, even if others do not see it. Religion arises at those human places in the universe where foreground and background lose their distinction, where the imagination and the mind and the heart become continuous with each other.

So why subordinate such experiences to mere believing? Why convert them into tinker-toy constructs that another person might quite easily reconfigure for some other use? After all, beliefs are merely choices that we make, ideas or notions that we can toss back and forth, or even throw **at** others in moments of self-righteousness. By asserting such beliefs, even with excessive passion or because they are backed up by some authority, what are we really doing? My belief is this and your belief is that. But what do any beliefs have to do with the way the world is or with where the world is going or with where the world came from? Behind and before our belief formulas there are relationships, elemental moments of the soul, subtle cords binding us to places and persons and events and memories that are laden with mystery and resonant with significance. Foreground relationships mediate those background relationships that beckon us to visions or hopes, to fears or exaltations, to feelings of being present to the mystery or being found in a lost universe. Turning those moments into beliefs--into propositions uttered only to protect us from the consequences or implications of other propositions--only dilutes them, simplifies them, sterilizes them.

It is, in my estimation, time to redefine religion--or rather, to recover the original definition--or better still, to reclaim the experience of those relationships that baffle us and keep us awake at night or at least wake us early in the morning. I am not really sure that I would venture a new formal definition, however. But I do know that the dictionary misses the point when it presumes that religion is defined exclusively as "belief in a superhuman power recognized as the creator and governor of the universe." The ways of living out a relationship with the universe, or with any natural or historic phase of that universe, so far exceed mere believing that I want to start back at the beginning of the human career and try to say it right this time.

But before I finish, let me be clear about two matters. I understand well enough that there may be no way to resist converting experience into belief, especially after the elemental experiences have been, so to speak, passed around. Eventually people will at least try to share such experiences until some version of them becomes common property.

For example, the foreground relationships with Jesus, Siddartha or Muhammad were for a few so overwhelming that they could hardly resist talking about them, trying to evoke in others some semblance of the experience. This seems especially true now-a-days, since the Christian "creedal paradigm" has become pervasive in defining religion in discussion that has spread through what Marshall McCluhan called the "global village." How and why that happened is a fascinating historical question. I do not want to attempt an answer here.

In any event, the impulse to formulate beliefs seems clearly to have overtaken historical, non-archaic societies--or at least those who presume to talk about them. But as soon as a tradition gives into the temptation of talking about believing as a way of expressing religious experience, the danger arises that the first relationships that defined individual and communal life may begin to fade or at least veer into confusion. But surely, whatever the reason, the farther one moves from the original moment, the more tenuous the subjective experience becomes, until it is only a pale imitation of the original. Eventually, I suppose, passionate talk about the relationship blurs into rhetorical utterances and finally it is, in order to preserve at least the memory, translated into evocative gestures and then into a formula that becomes the property of a cadre on its way to becoming an institution.

If this is an inevitable process--and the history of religion is replete with examples--then so be it. My fundamental hope is that we should not lose, or perhaps that we try to regain, some sense of those elemental relationships, both those in the foreground and those in the background of our consciousness. In my best judgment, those are the *ur*-moments in personal and in historic time, the primal psychic events, the original ecstasy, the authentic human intuition that binds us to an other, indeed, to the Other.[10]

My motive in all this is simply to try to find a way to **understand** religious experience that will preserve its elemental, pre-institutional origin! The fantasies and formulas that usurp our attention and divert our energies from such experienced relationships cannot possibly satisfy our existential longing or our ordinary desires to feel connected to the universe and to all other realities that mediate that connection.

Has the Time Come to Redefine Religion?

It is a terrible thought that our culture-laden discourse has become so imperious, so powerful in its influence on our conscience and consciousness that it will eventually lure us so far away from the elemental relationships I am talking about that not even the memory will survive. Indeed, we may eventually forget that we have forgotten the primal relationships as well as those in the foreground. It may even happen that foreground and background change places and the myriad connections that make us human fade into a myopic blur.

So I have argued that, before it is too late, at least a faithful remnant should make themselves aware of the time before religious traditions were politicized, to the time before those extended moments were overwhelmed by the temptation to define religious experience in creeds, in formulas of belief. Too quickly those pledges of allegiance turn into the heavy curtains that enclose us in certainty, and thereby deprive us of the mystery that is known, that is imagined in and through the most elemental experience of the human person-- relationships with an other and with the Other.

I wonder if I have, in any way, been persuasive in venturing a redefinition of religion? Driven equally by reason and passion, I have tried to construct a seaworthy craft on which to navigate the ocean of doubt whose tides may be washing into small inward seas where we live and wonder: where and why and how and what and, perhaps even, whether? What I tried to do was to marry the ghost of the elemental religious experience that haunts us to the spirit of the times in which we live. I have suggested that we redefine religion in such a way that we may regain connection with the original moment when the human person wakes up to relationships that baffle explanation but are still undeniable in their effect on how she or he lives in the universe. It is those very relationships that demand to be represented in the dramatic images of mythic tales to be told to and by the faithful.

Notes

1 *Belief, Language, and Experience* (Chicago: University of Chicago, 1972), p. 245, emphasis mine.

Religion and Mythology

2 Needham, p. 244.

3 Needham, p. 246.

4 John Hick and Paul F. Knitter, editors, (Maryknoll, NY, 1992), p. vii.

5 Hick and Knitter, "Religious Diversity, Historical Consciousness, and Christian Theology" by Gordon Kaufman, p. 9, emphasis mine.

6 *Ibid.,* p. 9.

7 *Op. Cit.*, p. 12.

8 William P. Barr, in a speech "The Judeo-Christian Tradition vs. Secularism," delivered at the Catholic League for Religious and Civil Rights, Washington, D.C., October 6, 1992. Refer to *Vital Speeches*, November 1, 1992. Emphasis mine.

9 Some may insist, of course, that religion is not a "quest" but an "arrival." From this perspective religious experience is best understood as "being found by" rather than "looking for" the answers to the "big questions." Still, the mythology of the hero dramatizes the journey in search of what is true, in pursuit of one's destiny. Rather than being a journey driven by curiosity and wonder, being religious may, by many conventions, mean knowing in one's heart that the questions have answers--and have been answered. I cannot argue with the conviction that certainty is "the gift of the spirit," though there are many who would find the "quest" metaphor more in tune with personal experience--and, perhaps, even with historical experience.

10 See Rudolph Otto, *The Idea of the Holy*, trans. John H. Harvey, revised with additions (London: Oxford University Press, 1936).

PART II
:
MYTHOLOGY

CHAPTER I

MYTHMAKING AS A HABIT OF MIND
:
FIRST CONSIDERATIONS

So far I have argued that religion and mythology have lived out a marriage that is primeval and persistent. If we could avoid the imperious influence of the "belief paradigm" in all manner of religious discourse, we might better understand the historic reciprocity of mythmaking and religious experience. Both dramatize and celebrate the relationships of human beings and communities to the historical and natural familiarities of the world. Also if we could avoid the post-Enlightenment bias against myths that sees them as failed explanations of phenomena, we might be able, at last, to appreciate this primal union of devotion and storytelling, of awe and intimacy, of relationships and imagination,--of religion and mythology.

In Part I, Chapter I, I ventured to redefine religion as grounded in relationships. Now I want to redefine myths so as to expose the legitimate basis of the marriage that these two wonders of human experience have enjoyed "from the beginning." This will not be a light task, of course, since by now, at least among professional and casual skeptics alike, our ideas about myth and religion have been virtually overwhelmed by a presumptive devotion to Science and Rationality. Neither party to this union, we are tempted to suppose, qualifies as either scientific or rational. So, I must be candid. I have already proposed a perspective on religion that challenges the learned impulse to dismiss it as either archaic or, even worse, constituted only by what

Religion and Mythology

folks believe. Now I want to reconsider the very nature of mythology, the other party to this original marriage.

Since this issue is perhaps more practical than abstract, I am unwilling to divorce persuasion from analysis. Myths have to do with that great conundrum that haunts human awareness: the dynamic relationship between perceived chaos and the human impulse to order our experience of the world. The implications and the consequences of this circumstance are relentlessly pragmatic as well as existential and metaphysical.

The sheer presence in our past and in our present of myths and mythologies should provoke us to understand them with an eye to restore some of the power that the terms seems to have lost. To this end I want to work out a hermeneutic of mythmaking. As the argument advances, we shall think of mythologies themselves as **artifacts**, though I trust that the implications of that label will be understood simply as having to do with the fact that myths survive over time, even while subject to changes of content and interpretation. Even though mythologies may seem to be embedded in a lost past, we must find a way to recognize them as authentic, albeit disguised, **knowledge** useful in any present . Even though artifacts may often be antiques, we should resist the temptation to dismiss them as antiquated.

The first move in that direction is to think of mythmaking as a **habit of mind**. "Habit" suggests "emotions" and "behavior"; "mind" suggests "thinking" and "knowing." A "habit of mind" involves processes that are comprehensively "mental," neither exclusively cognitive nor obsessively passionate. If mythmaking is a habit of human beings, then it repeats itself. Having once "imagined" human experience, certain persons will persist in doing just that even in our own time. Many, however, locked as they are in the not-so-enormous room of the present, prefer to disdain mythmaking and to respond to myths in a dismissive manner, to see only falsehoods where ancient persons meant to conjure stories rather than pretend to explanations.

In the end, the best we can do in responding to the Myth Family[1] is to appreciate its eccentricities and hope that it will survive to assist our understanding of our ancestors **and** of ourselves, and to help us to appreciate why religious experience entered into an alliance with mythmaking that is both historic and historical.

Mythmaking As A Habit Of Mind

Like most other human behaviors, mythmaking generates and reflects human values. That is precisely why I want to argue for "appreciating" it. The term clearly implies a reference to "value." When a piece of property "appreciates," the meaning is that its (market) value increases. So, I want to try to learn how to **value** mythmaking as an integral part of the human enterprise and also to discover how mythmaking itself affects the human capacity for experience. I shall approach the mythmaking process itself as a mode of cognition that operated powerfully in the past and even now continues to give the mind an advantage in its everlasting wrestle with the sheer complexity of being human in an ambient world.

I referred above to "a hermeneutic of mythmaking." Hermeneutics, as the science of interpretation, should address the question of how we make sense of the remnants of that habit of mind that created worlds, gods and heroes, deeds and events that can best be described as "imaginative." How shall we understand the process as it continues to enchant and to inform even those who believe that it can only produce lies and deceptions?[2]

How do we approach a stranger whose behavior and person intrigue us? With announcements of our certainties? or in a posture of dialogue? The answer is obvious. And that is how I propose that we approach mythologies--anticipating dialogue with the mythmakers, prompting conversations with them and with the artifactual stories they have left behind. The values and allusions to experience projected by and inherent in myths may then begin to show themselves, and the imagination may again be recognizable as a viable--and valid--way of knowing what sense our experience carries with it.

On the frontispiece of his book, *The Labyrinth of Solitude*, Octavio Paz quotes Antonio Machado:

> The other does not exist: this is rational faith, the incurable belief of human reason. Identity = reality, as if in the end, everything must necessarily and absolutely be one and the same. *But the other refuses to disappear; it subsists, it persists; it is the hard bone on which reason breaks its teeth.* Abel Martin, with a poetic faith as human as rational faith, believed in the other, "the

essential Heterogeneity of being," in what might be called the incurable otherness from which oneness must always suffer.[3]

The mythmaker confronts "the essential Heterogeneity of being"; he breaks his teeth on it, but when he cries out in pain, he tells a story. He shapes his experience of the hard other as a "plot," a mythic scenario that we should not pretend works as an empirical presentation of reality. But if it does not work that way, how does it work, what does it do? Trying to answer these questions is the aim of what follows. First we shall look around to discern what has been said and what is currently being said about interpreting mythology. Then we shall venture to develop and to refine a hermeneutic of mythmaking. In this we shall try to be sensitive to what the imagination was doing when it created those cultural artifacts that still survive, and appreciative of what it is now: an unbreakable habit of mind that represents human experience without explaining it. The mythmaker was and is able still "to imagine" what we now prefer--or presume--"to know."

To take the decisive step in this approach, we should be prepared to ask what myths are **and** what they do. We shall make our way to the following answer: *Myths are stories that render experience intelligible in a dramatic mode.* The implications of that critical judgment are the interest of this essay. And in the search for those implications, we shall try to keep in focus the judgment that the religious experience of relationship is quite susceptible to being taken up by the mythmaking imagination.

Notes

1   I intend this trope merely as a rhetorical gesture. With it I refer to that cluster of terms that derive from the root, *mythos*: myth, mythic, mythical, mythmaker, mythmaking, mythopoesis. Consulting any dictionary, one will find a range of usage that confuses ordinary diction: from "a traditional story originating in a pre-literate society" to "a notion based more on tradition or convenience than on fact." By invoking the image of a "Myth Family," I mean to acknowledge the clutter that surrounds the term and, in the essay, to develop a more consistent usage that appreciates both the ancient and the contemporary

manifestations of mythmaking. As the reader will see, I am concerned with the "identity crisis" of that "family." Since we find ourselves living in "the psychological society," this enterprise seems more than appropriate.

2   The examples of this kind of usage for "myth" are legion. One that recently came to hand was in the *Democratic Left* (July/August, 1992) in an article with the title, "The Myth of Dependence: Why Welfare Works and Workfare Fails" (by Cloward and Piven). The "argument" is clearly stated in the conclusion of the article: "Welfare does not generate dependency." Hence, the belief that "welfare" has negative effects on the lifestyle of the "poor" is simply wrong; it is a "myth." Any sympathetic use of the concept of "myth" is quite infrequent among journalists and other "popular" writers. Later in the essay I cite one of those rare examples of non-pejorative use by William Greider in his book, *Who Will Tell the People*.

3   (New York: Grove Press, 1961). Emphasis mine.

CHAPTER II

MYTHMAKING AS A HABIT OF MIND : CIRCUMSPECTION

Wendy Doniger O'Flaherty insists that myths are communal stories.[1] There are many, on the other hand, who insist that narratives satisfy a mostly personal need for intelligibility. When we try to make sense of our lives, however, we do not stare into a mirror to recite our tales. Our "narratives" are indeed subject to conventions; that is, our stories must satisfy a community's expectations. Such stories must be told so that they are recognizable to more than one person. They are meant to engage others. Myths, in a certain sense, make up the "autobiography" of a community. They preserve memories, collective and individual; they allow us to project the past into the future; and, most urgently, they try to make sense of a wide range of real experience.

What, then, is the peculiar strategy by which the story tellers of a community make sense of life as personal experience and as the consciousness of a community embedded at the same time in the natural, the historical and the cosmic order? In the arena of much public discourse, such a question seem almost irrelevant. Myths are not acknowledged with appreciation of their power to order the world or our minds; something has happened to the very notion of myth to obscure both its one-time meaning and its on-going presence. Its authority to interpret or to represent experience has been eroded.

After centuries, perhaps even millennia, of being useful to the psychological and historical needs of rulers, priests and people, the very notion of "myth" now suffers an identity crisis. We can no longer be sure precisely what a myth is. In magazines, newspapers and in common parlance, myth is referred to casually and incidentally as though it were self-evidently foolish. Folks in the "modern world" hardly need to pretend the existence of fabled gods and bizarre events. A myth seems to have no more "reality" than a show conjured on TV to distract the lazy minds of people who have lost touch with themselves and with others in the world we now all inhabit. Mythic characters and scenarios exist only in the make-believe settings of lost civilizations. A myth is now the lie that deceives those who should know better; it is what we now mean by propaganda, often deceitful, always misleading.

Myths, however, continue to haunt our intellectual machinery. There is a real ghost in that machine that howls or whispers in our many modes of discourse. But do ghosts really exist? Only the befuddled mind will allow itself to believe in such a superannuated relic. Still, we cannot quite bring ourselves to dismiss myths out of hand. Perhaps, we may suspect, some validity still clings to them, despite the fact that they persist only as recluses hidden in the attic where they molder unawares in their senility. We seem unable to forget what myths used to be and do, though we are not quite sure that their tasks were ever really necessary. Useful, yes, but more as evidence of dreams than of real knowledge. They may be hauled out annually to justify the inauguration of kings who no longer rule. The uses to which myth have been put are legion, so prolific, in fact, that the concept has lost its moorings in literature and in history. It drifts among psychologies while anthropologists examine it and journalists abuse it.

For example, we can now be sure that a myth is a *bona fide* lie concocted to subvert the politically naive. One can recognize this complex usage in Andrew Kopkind's article in *The Nation* with the obvious title, "*JFK*: The Myth."[2] In a commentary on Oliver Stone's film, *JFK*, Kopkind observed that "(Stone's) method is to substitute another myth--consistent, compelling and just a little unconvincing--for the 'official' one that seems to have been a comfort for so long but is so shot full of holes by now that it can barely float." In qualifying "official," Kopkind exposes the popular bias by applying "myth" to a public story.

For more than thirty years we denizens of the body social have, for the most part, been hoodwinked by a particular version of the actors and of the events in the "national tragedy" that intruded itself into our consciousness in November, 1963. Now a movie has produced a substitute version, another interpretation. Kopkind comments that "It was a great film and brilliant *propaganda*, which is to say, what movies

Circumspection

ought to be."[3] Why "propaganda," especially in its pejorative sense of another "lie," another contrivance? The assumption is that the reality of that event continues to elude us until that fateful day when "the 'truth' will set us free"? So even in the sophisticated journalism of *The Nation*, myths have the reputation of being falsehoods. In the case of the film *JFK*, the new myth is a provocative and responsible falsehood: Kopkind concludes that Oliver Stone (the director) "has done a great service by recasting the idols in the heart of the temple." But with regard to the "reality," his "recasting of idols" has provided only one more contrivance to compensate us for enduring the taunting by a communal memory that could, if it wanted to (and if, presumably, we wanted it to), reveal its "truth." So we have here a powerful example of, at best, the equivocal use of the concept of "myth."

Let's indulge Kopkind one more time:

> For virtually every American alive and conscious of a social reality in November 1963, the assassination forms the central political myth of the public world. The myth is in the matrix of the national experience, etched by television and consecrated by ritual, and no amount of political science will demystify the memory of murder.

Note the rhetorical strategy. The "political myth" is "etched" in our collective mind. Not even political *science* can erase ("demystify") it. Still, in the journalistic context, both the "official" and the cinematic versions are "myths," and hence not bona fide explanations of what **really** happened. Individually and collectively, we live with a lie, whether contrived for our entertainment or as part of a counter-conspiracy in social control.

So myths seem unable to shake off the reputation that journalists have devised for them. Beyond journalism, however, one finds still other usages that currently add to the confusion suffered by myth.

On the one hand, myths simultaneously entertain us and deceive us. They seem to be lies that betray us more than they enchant us. On the other hand, if we grasped the human condition better than we seem able to, we would hear "the cry for myth" that Rollo May[4] listens to from the privileged chair of the therapist. From there May realizes that collectively we have allowed the "ancient myths" to fall into disrepair--

Religion and Mythology

and many of us now suffer unexpected deprivations amid the dilapidation.

Obviously, we have thrown out the baby with the bath. In ridding ourselves of the primitive fantasies of ancient civilizations and aboriginal societies, we have also deprived ourselves of a compass for navigating in our "morally confusing world." Rollo May assures us that "Myth making is essential in gaining mental health, and the compassionate therapist will not discourage it. Indeed," he continues, " the very birth and proliferation of psychotherapy in our contemporary age were called forth by the disintegration of our myths."[5] It is still not clear what relation these therapeutic stories have to "reality." But, if they contribute to our psychological well-being, surely they have power in the confines of our "mental world" even if they lack validity in the "outside world" into which our mind normally reaches. Rollo May further contributes to the uncertainty of the concept by quoting Freud, in his correspondence with Einstein:

> "It may perhaps seem to you as though our theories are a kind of mythology. . . . But does not every science come in the end to a kind of mythology like this? Cannot the same be said today of your own Physics?"[6]

Freud, the godfather of the psychological expose, here seems to have an intuition of the confusion--and the longing--that eventually forces itself on the concept of myth. It is at least **like** a theory, and we know in the "age of science" that theories are indispensable tools in mastering the **natural** world where the human psyche cavorts on an equal footing with molecules, chimpanzees and dahlias. Is it possible, then, to justify an interest in, if not a commitment to, myth recognized as an accidental surrogate in the quest for scientific knowledge?

But the forest of meaning through which "myth" must find its way home grows even denser. In 1986, Peter Berger wrote *The Capitalist Revolution: Fifty Propositions about Prosperity, Equality, And Liberty*.[7] In the book, Berger marries polemic and analysis, trying to find room for the contribution of the social sciences to public policy. In a climactic chapter, Berger formulates his fiftieth proposition as follows:

Circumspection

> *Socialism, in addition to being a set of political programs and the source of social-scientific interpretations, is also one of the most powerful myths of the contemporary era; to the extent that socialism retains this* mythic quality, *it cannot be disconfirmed by empirical evidence in the minds of its adherents.*[8]

So myths live (operate) in a world immune to "empirical evidence." Berger bears down on the point even more strongly: ". . . perhaps it is even possible to falsify Marxism as a body of theory; it is *not* possible to falsify Marxism (or socialism in general) as a mythic vision of human hope."[9] Part of the argument of the book is that "capitalism" is not susceptible to such mythical (i.e., ideological) apologetics. Be that as it may, in this argument, "myth" runs on a track at least parallel to ideology. Myths dramatize or, in some other obscure way, justify the peculiar ideas that make up "socialism" as a historical phenomenon. Berger puts the finishing touches to his analysis in this way: "By contrast with the mythopoetic productivity of socialism, capitalism is and always has been mythically deprived."[10] Whether, in Berger's analysis, this deprivation is capitalism's virtue or its weakness, whether socialism's susceptibility to myth is its weakness or its virtue, I leave up to the reader who wants to pursue the analysis. I am satisfied simply to have pointed out that the concept of myth has wandered into great public confusion, driven there by its exploitation by Peter Berger's sociological escapades.

So far we have considered myth's functions by indicating what myth does to us and what we do with myth. But there are still other approaches to making sense of these apparently archaic remnants of bygone worlds. Quite recently, Joseph Campbell has captured popular (and perhaps also scholarly) attention by coming to mythmaking from still a different angle. If Campbell has a partnership with any of the other approaches discussed above, it would be with Rollo May. There is, however, a difference. May sees mythology as therapeutic. Campbell, on the one hand, sees it as a psychological phenomenon in itself and, as such, having curative potential. On the other hand, however, he is more interested in why and how the human mind or spirit generates mythologies. For Campbell, myth provides the

Religion and Mythology

expressive device that provokes and fulfills the mind's romance with itself.

In the concluding essay of an anthology of his writings, *Myths To Live By*,[11] he makes the following observations:

> For it is simply a fact--as I believe we have all now got to concede--that mythologies and their deities are productions and projections of the psyche.[12]

Toward the end of the same essay, he asserts:

> Now it strikes me as evident through all this that the imagery of mythology, stemming as it does from the psyche and reflecting back to the same, represents in its various inflections various stages or degrees of the opening of ego-consciousness toward the prospect of what Aldous Huxley has . . . called Mind at Large.[13]

Now this same psyche that gives rise to universal images is itself in touch with a larger reality. Campbell quotes Plato in the *Timaeus* to make the point:

> ". . . there is only one way in which one being can serve another, and this is by giving him his proper nourishment and motion: and the motions that are akin to the divine principle within us are the thoughts and revolutions of the universe."[14]

Those familiar with the thought of Carl Jung, of course, will hear its echoes in Campbell. Earlier in the essay under discussion, and throughout his writing, Campbell establishes this dependency: ". . . all serious students of psychology and of comparative religions today, have recognized and hold that the forms of myth and the figures of myth are of the nature essentially of dream."[15] The reliance on Jung (and to a lesser degree, on Freud) is quite clear. Throughout humanity, the essential dreams are the same, only their "forms," the particulars of their expression, differ. So by familiarizing ourselves with the mythologies of the world we get the definitive clue to "...[the psyche's] structure, its order and its forces, in symbolic terms."[16]

Given the size of Campbell on the horizon of mythological study, we might let him finish his own argument:

Circumspection

> I have thought about this problem a good deal and have come to the conclusion that when the symbolic forms in which wisdom-lore has been everywhere embodied are interpreted not as referring primarily to any supposed or even actual historical personages or events but **psychologically**, properly "spiritually," as referring to the inward potentials of our species, there then appears through all something that can be properly termed a *philosophia perennis* of the human race, which, however, is lost to view when the texts are interpreted literally, as history in the usual ways of harshly orthodox thought.[17]

Myth, then, is the romantic song that the psyche sings to itself, about itself. Myths celebrate the "Inward Journey," as the psyche swims or founders in "the tides and undertows of our inward sea."[18] But it also celebrates the "Outward Journey,"[19] the adventure of the universal voyager, "the hero with a thousand faces" in search of the soul of the cosmos itself, while winning his own redemption. Myths commemorate the entry into the soul's own labyrinth **and** the escape to the Moon and the heavens beyond. The mythologies of the world, then, are all about the same thing: the search for the Self and Self-realization.

From a quite different quarter, myth is confronted with still other "definitions" of itself. Mircea Eliade has tried to construct a consistent interpretation of myth, especially as found in "archaic societies." In his contribution to the World Perspectives series, Eliade ventures this definition:

> Myth narrates a sacred history; it relates an event that took place in primordial Time, the fabled time of the "beginnings." In other words, myth tells how, through the deeds of Supernatural Beings, a reality came into existence, be it the whole of reality, the Cosmos, or only a fragment of reality--an island, a species of plant, a particular kind of human behavior, an institution.[20]

Also in the same book he comments favorably on Bronislav Malinowski's notion of myth as a charter that legitimates a society's beliefs and practices. But when we try to grasp Eliade's way of understanding myths, we may want to note the orthography of the statement above.

Religion and Mythology

The capitalization of (primordial) "Time" cannot be capricious. Indeed Eliade has written extensively about "the myth of the eternal return." For him "Time" is not the ordinary linear process that sweeps events relentlessly forward through "history." "Time" is a function of the sacred cosmos, its Eternity, in which the sacred drama forever overwhelms the potentialities of the profane World. From this perspective, "Myth tells only of that which *really* happened, which manifested itself completely."[21] Eliade clearly has a view of myth as the script of events "beyond the natural;" that is, myth reveals the metaphysical realities otherwise hidden from ordinary view.

> In short, myths describe the various and sometimes dramatic breakthroughs of the sacred (or the "supernatural") into the World. It is this sudden breakthrough of the sacred that really *establishes* the World and makes it what it is today. Furthermore, it is as a result of the intervention of Supernatural Beings that man himself is what he is today, a mortal, sexed, and cultural being.[22]

In order to establish himself in relation to the rest of contemporary philosophy, Eliade in effect "calls the bluff" of the existentialists: "For *homo religiosus* the essential precedes existence."[23] Myth, then, functions to convey the intuitions of archaic (and perhaps of modern) "man" and thereby throws light not so much on the psychic labyrinth as on the cosmic landscape.

On the other hand, from still another direction, Claude Lévi-Strauss finds myth's true vocation in life as a coded message, "a single unitary message, inherent in the architecture of the human mind."[24] Mythologies, then, are something like "algebraic formulas,"[25] revealing the structure of experience and necessarily reflecting the structure of thought tied to language. The structure both of experience and of thought yields best to a "binary" analysis. The pairs that our consciousness reveals to us are legion: the raw and the cooked, society and nature, male and female, light and darkness, fresh and corrupt, moist and burnt, and so forth. Such "binary opposites" are what our language permits us to "think" and the resolution of those opposites is what the native "*bricoler*"[26] accomplishes in mythmaking. The myths are ingenious stories--or rather arrays of stories--that are structured by the formative process of cognition driving toward some resolution of these oppositions. According to Lévi-Strauss, what is universal about any myth is not its content but its source in "the inbuilt logic of a nonrational kind."[27]

In volume II of *Mythologiques*, Lévi-Strauss reveals his own philosophical penchant (bias):

> . . . mythical thought surpasses itself and contemplates, beyond images still clinging to concrete experience, a world of concepts. . . (defined) no longer by reference to an external reality, but according to their own mutual affinities or incompatibilities manifested in the *architecture of the spirit.*."[28]

Responding to what he recognizes in Lévi-Strauss as a "Platonist mood," G. S. Kirk suggests:

> By "spirit," Lévi-Strauss seems to mean the very structure of the human mind, which is the same all over the world, among illiterate tribesmen and the supposedly civilized: an innate tendency to work in certain ways, notably by a process of binary analysis.[29]

When all is said and done in the many efforts to respond to the seminal arguments of Lévi-Strauss, G. S. Kirk's interpretation seems cogent enough: "To use language which Lévi-Strauss does not permit himself (because it is too simple?), man has a tendency to reduce the manifold world of his experience to an orderly system whose operation he can to some extent predict."[30] This, it seems, is the upshot of Lévi-Strauss' structuralist analysis of mythmaking.

In that uncertain territory between the human psyche and history, many intellectual adventurers have tried to find their way. We have tried to identify only some of the most conspicuous efforts. These and many others form a company of explorers too numerous to mention, all ranging along the philosophical course as though they were alone: semioticists and psychologists, historians and linguists, literary critics and religionists, poets and novelists, anthropologists and classicists, and on and on. So, myths are entertainment, propaganda, therapy, theory, ideology, coded messages, the effusion of religious experience, and more. Surely, one of the most heroic and dispassionate responses to this endless variety in the study of mythology is William G. Doty's *Mythography*.[31] This and other studies of myth, along with the anthologies of articles[32] trying to look behind the veil of myths, all threaten to inflict a massive "identity crisis" on what I am tempted to call the "Myth Family."

With this trope I intend only to refer to that cluster of terms that derive from the root *mythos* myth, mythic, mythical, mythmaker, mythmaking (mythopoesis). Consulting any dictionary, one will find a range of usage that confuses ordinary diction: from "a traditional story originating in pre-literate society" to "a notion based more on tradition or convenience than on fact." By invoking the image of a "Myth Family," I mean to acknowledge the clutter that surrounds the term and, in what follows, to develop a more consistent usage that appreciates both the ancient and the contemporary manifestations of mythmaking. As the reader has seen, I am concerned with the "identity crisis" of that "family." Since we find ourselves living in "the psychological society," this enterprise seems more than appropriate.

In face of this crisis, perhaps, one more effort in the direction of a hermeneutic of mythmaking can be tolerated. I hope what follows is sensitive, though not slavishly beholden, to the vast array of scholarship on this subject. In its own way it has a single-minded suggestion to make. This desire to simplify the enterprise may exacerbate the confusion--or it may lead us to discover a window that has not yet been opened onto the vast House of Myth.

Notes

1   See especially Wendy Doniger O'Flaherty, *Other People's Myths: The Cave of Echoes* (New York: Macmillan Publishing Co: New York, 1988).

2   20 January 1991.

3   Emphasis mine.

4   Rollo May, *The Cry For Myth* (New York: W. W. Norton Co. 1991).

5   May, p. 15.

Circumspection

6   Quoted on p. 11.

7   Peter Berger (New York: Basic Books, Inc. 1986).

8   Berger, p. 204.

9   Berger, p. 205.

10 *Ibid.*

11 Joseph Campbell, *Myths To Live By* (New York: Bantam edition, pub. June, 1973).

12 Campbell, "Envoy: Nor More Horizons," p. 261.

13 Campbell, p. 272.

14 Campbell, p. 273.

15 Campbell, p. 261. Campbell is also sympathetic with Jung's notion of the "archetypes" that Jung sees repeating themselves in dreams (which he calls the myths of individuals) and in traditional myths (which he calls the dreams of the society). Campbell commits himself to this critical idea in his *Hero With A Thousand Faces* and in the several volumes of his *magnum opus*, *The Masks of God*.

16 *Ibid.*

17 Campbell, p. 264.

18 "Schizophrenia--The Inward Journey," p. 224.

19 See "The Moon Walk--The Outward Journey," pp. 240-257.

20 *Myth and Reality*, trans. Hillard R. Task (New York: Harper and Row, 1963), p. 6.

21 Eliade, p. 6.

22 *Ibid.*

23 Eliade, p. 92. Compare Sartre's famous formulation to the effect that "existence precedes essence."

24 Edmund Leach, *Claude Lévi-Strauss* (New York: Viking Press, 1970), p. 65.

25 One is tempted here to invoke the current notion of the *algorithm* to enlarge this paradigm for what myths are and how they operate.

26 In *The Savage Mind* (Chicago: University of Chicago Press, 1966) Lévi-Strauss explains this metaphor: "The characteristic feature of mythical thought is that it expresses itself by means of a heterogeneous repertoire [i.e., *bricolage*] which, even if extensive, is nevertheless limited. [Mythical thought] has to use this repertoire, however, whatever the task in hand because it has nothing else at its disposal. Mythical thought is therefore a kind of intellectual *'bricolage'* . . . ." (p. 17). *Bricoler* is simply the agent of *bricolage*.

27 Leach, p. 58.

28 Quoted in G. S. Kirk, *Myth: Its Meaning and Functions in Ancient and Other Cultures* (Berkeley and Los Angeles: University of California, 1970), p. 45. Emphasis mine.

29 Kirk, p. 45.

30 Kirk, p. 47.

31 (University, Alabama: University of Alabama Press:, 1986). For an earlier attempt to review the variety of approaches to the study of mythology, see Raphael Patai, *Myth and Modern Man* (New Jersey: Prentice Hall:, 1972). This book is less encyclopedic than Doty's book, and it undertakes to see mythmaking as both a historical as well as a contemporary enterprise.

32 Thomas A. Sebeok, ed. *Myth: A Symposium* (Bloomington: Indiana University Press, 1958). Henry A. Murray, ed., *Myth and Mythmaking* (Boston: Beacon, 1959, 1959). John Middleton, ed., *Myth and Cosmos, Readings in Mythology and Symbolism* (New

Circumspection

York:Doubleday, 1967). Pierre Maranda, ed., *Mythology: Selected Readings* (Penguin: Baltimore, 1972).

CHAPTER III

MYTHMAKING AS A HABIT OF MIND : IMAGINING HOW MYTHS ARE MADE

Hadrian's Wall, the Great Wall of China, the Berlin Wall were more than feats of engineering. They were also monuments, mythic structures that spoke of the marriage of political power with xenophobia. They were protective barriers in the landscape and mythic symbols curled up behind the mind's eye. Such walls are virtual myths, and many myths may confront us as virtual walls. The material out of which walls may be made is quite irrelevant, whether stone or wood--or words. The concern of this essay is to look at myth as something like a wall that stands between us and some apparently inaccessible experience. First, however, we should consider how many ways there are to respond to the presence of a "real" wall.

First, one could deny its presence and thereby discount whatever of interest may lie on the other side, or one might take a more aggressive approach. A person might climb over the wall or may organize an expedition to go around it, if we assume that its ends are not in sight and there is no available information as to the extent of the wall. We could try to dig under the wall, though the unknown depth of its foundation may discourage this strategy. One act of sanity in the presence of a wall might be to paint a mural across its surface, decorating it with a portrait of immediate interests or fascinations. Or one may simply say, "There is a wall," and go about the business that was momentarily interrupted.

These responses, however, do not exhaust our possibilities. For instance, we could declare the wall off limits to anyone who knows about it. We could organize a demolition squad, either to tear it down or at least to breach the wall. We might even be satisfied merely to drill a hole through the wall, assuming, of course, that the material is not impervious. Finally, one could mount a balloon to fly over the wall, leaving it in tact to taunt others with its presence.

Before or after any of these responses, one may inaugurate legal action (or maybe only a friendly inquiry) to determine whose wall it is and how it got there--and why it is there obstructing our curiosity as well as our progress. In that process, of course, we might discover that the wall bears no relation to any current interest. It might be there, independent of our frustration or of our curiosity.

Imagine that an artifactual myth is a wall. Our encounter with a "real" wall may in most respects be analogous to our responses to that cultural phenomenon. Amid all the possibilities, one thing is clear: myths confront us by their very presence, while their historical or psychological origins at least initially may baffle us. Most of us do not have a predetermined repertoire of responses to what convention calls a "myth." All of the above are possible and perhaps our ingenuity may discover still other options.

Initially, however, myths are, for us in this part of the twentieth century, virtual or even real walls. We shall not here play out **all** the possible strategies in response to that perspective. I am satisfied merely to recognize myth as an apparent obstruction requiring ingenious responses--with, however, one proviso: We may **not** presume to demolish the wall. Circle it, vault it, burrow under it, crash into it; deny it, subject it to scrutiny and study; even write its history and establish the legal basis of its presence. But we may not blow it up or follow any other tactic aimed at obliterating it. We may practice denial, but that strategy cannot last forever. Sooner or later myth confronts us, either as ruined artifact or as a piece of machinery still operating.

Of course, there is an irony in this analogy that we have not yet noticed. A wall has two sides. From the other side, the wall merely establishes the boundaries of a world. From our side, especially if the wall is a myth, it appears to be hiding something or it seems to be there to keep us out. It is revealing to think of all cross-cultural communication as having to negotiate an encounter with a wall. From our side it may be a challenge or an insult; from the other it is the perimeter, the frontier that defines a world.

In the previous chapter we identified the variety of contexts in which myths seem to operate. We explored many, though certainly not

Imagining: How Myths Are Made

all, avenues of approach to myth. Here we have tried to see it as a "wall," albeit with two sides. It inflicts upon us the realization that "our side" and the "other side" mutually create each other. What is an obstacle from one side may be a boundary from the other side. Surely, our approach to myth must be sensitive to this dilemma.

But myth is also a historical datum, an unavoidable, though often puzzling, artifact. There is, however, a problem with this judgment: we may presume that "artifacts" are merely relics of a past with no contemporary viability or use. The pyramids that currently intrigue tourists were once (and in some sense, still are) royal tombs. Compare the Sears Tower or the World Trade Center or the Swedegon Pagoda. Imagine a time when these also will be primarily tourist attractions, deprived of their original practical use. Or take potsherds for another example of "artifact." It is not as though we were no longer making pots or that pots were merely relics of a time out of mind. In track and field, hurling the javelin is still an event, even though few successful battles are fought with spears. The point is not obvious, but it is important for my argument. People can still sit on antique chairs or drive old cars. Antiquity does not translate as irrelevance or inaccessibility. An artifact, by being an artifact, is not automatically consigned to quaint oblivion. What we used to use we still use, though many changes may have modified the artifacts so thoroughly that we do not easily recognize the continuity--indeed, the sameness--of the objects.

The first thing we must do if we want to appreciate myth is to refuse to use the term itself dismissively. Antiques and artifacts were once useful and valuable in their own right, and now they may be powerful and interesting under different circumstances. "It's only a myth. . . " will not do as a response to those artifactual tales, any more than, "It's **only** a chair or pyramid, a foundation or stone ax, or even a skull or femur," also will not do as a response to the material remnants of antiquity. For we still have our chairs and towers and pottery, themselves in process of becoming artifacts. In the meanwhile, they do a day's work. So does myth do a day's work, though maybe not precisely the work it used to do. But, I shall argue, there are myths still being manufactured that are eligible eventually to become artifacts in our repertoire of self-understanding.

Religion and Mythology

If I have a single motive in this argument, it is this: I am anxious to replace a **dismissive**, essentially negative response to myth with an appreciative approach. We are still making myths just as we are still building pyramids and manufacturing chairs and pots and writing on something like clay tablets. It confuses both people and reality when we read the following:

> **Myth**: Welfare programs encourage teenage pregnancy.
> **Fact**: The stingiest program, in Mississippi, has the highest rate of unwed births while the most generous, in Minnesota, has the lowest.[1]

The common (popular) use of "myth" indicated in this promotional ad is typical. Clearly, Americans entertain mostly "myths" about the social behaviors referred to in the ad copy. That is to say, they have learned only falsehoods about the relationship of welfare programs and teenage pregnancy. The book being promoted will not so much interpret the "myths," as it will reveal the "truth" about otherwise dissociated social phenomena. The entire ad, of course, elaborates other such disparities and false correlations between "myth" and "fact."

This dismissive or negative use of "myth" carries with it the implication that Zeus was a primitive hoax, that there **really** was no Gilgamesh or Amaterasu or Vainomoinen; no such place as Xbalba or Mt. Meru; no such time as the Dreamtime; no dismembering of the primeval dragon or the sweating of the frost giant. Just as Americans are mistaken about the response of teenagers to welfare, so all those "ancients" were deluded about the objects of their "beliefs." We can now purge ourselves of religious fantasies; we can now check out our cosmologies and technologies; we can now "explain" what primitive people could only imagine. We live in a post-mythological age and thereby assume the privilege of denigrating the myths of the past and denying that we are still relying on those "old ways of thinking."

No one can deny that this use of "myth" is prevalent. We find one of a myriad of examples in the title of a book published in 1988: *Legends, Lies & Cherished Myths of American History.*[2] The promotional responses that the book evoked are as telling as the argument of the text itself. One review declares that this is "an

Imagining: How Myths Are Made

entertaining compendium of things that everyone knows but just aren't so." Another issues this compliment: "[Shenkman] tells us the truth about all the tall tales of American history that our school teachers always touted." Fact and myth are clearly polar opposites; one must yield to the other. We no longer need to be mislead by "our cherished bunk." Clearly, the merit of this book lies in its separating fact from "fiction." That distinction, it is assumed, is a good one to make in a society that prides itself on its relentless pragmatism and on its "scientific" empiricism.

How the very notion of "myth" was purged of its original appreciative meaning and converted to this kind of trivial usage is a complicated story. But even for that story, I am sure, there is not a single version. Others have tried to reconstruct it, but I find it not especially pertinent. The conversion is a *fait accompli* and I would rather work not so much to restore a presumably original meaning but to press forward toward a refinement of a usage that both responds to the kinds of interpretations we have already reviewed and to develop a couple of new angles from which we might approach the territory of mythology.

I have already hinted at the first phase of this enterprise. Myths are artifacts; that is, they are things skillfully made.[3] A certain connotation, however, has attached itself to the word: something made, "especially . . . of archeological or historical interest"--and therefore not of immediate or contemporary relevance. But there is nothing in the history of the word that forbids a more generous usage. An artifact is something skillfully made, whenever it was made. Some anthropologists used to devise Latin adjectives for *homo* in order to identify what was distinctively "human." One of the constructs was *homo faber*, suggesting that a species was "homo" by virtue of its being "faber," that is, a creature that could "fabricate" devices out of available materials. By this quaint definition, it is one expression of the distinctively human enterprise to "fabricate" things such as tools, buildings, jewelry and the like. Certainly, the variety of things that humans have made and continue to make are beyond number. And we need not separate them into things past and present. To be human is to fabricate--and the list of things made is inexhaustible.

Religion and Mythology

Surely, one of the artifacts that humans used to make is myths and one of the artifacts that humans continue to make is myths. By the simplest definition, then, myths are *stories that render experience intelligible in a dramatic mode.* Our immediate reluctance to concede the intelligibility rendered in the antique stories is, I believe, a failure of appreciation. We cannot, shadowed by fear of propaganda, define myth as deceitful or silly contrivance and then import that definition to account for a myth's original function. Would an archeologist belittle the "crude" oil lamps excavated at some level of a tell as not adequate to lighting a modern office building? The question is rhetorical, of course. The classical--or any mythology--is intelligible in a certain context, just as is any artifact. And since we know that material artifacts are still being "fabricated," we should be suspicious that myth is still being "imagined."

Think of a particular myth that is a fragment of familiar memory. Think of that myth as a lock that needs a key. What is the key? What is the question that you can ask the myth? We are still hoping that astrophysicists will "unlock" the mystery of the universe or that chemists will find a way to tease open the cornucopia of natural materials found in the rain forests of the world. We might practice the same courtesy toward mythmakers. How did they unlock the "mystery" of their experience--before social or natural sciences were invented?

I propose that we ask precisely this question in this way: How does one "imagine" experience? It should not require too strenuous an effort to use that verb, "to imagine," in a way analogous to the way one would apply the verb "to know." Perhaps we have been distracted by the abundance of ways that we can talk about "cognition." How many "cognitive modalities" are there anyway? I want to argue that they all arrange themselves along a continuum of application. In order to talk about myth, then, we should find an appropriate vocabulary somewhere along that continuum.

If we operate in the popular Campbellesque manner, we might search for the psychological reference or component in a particular myth. That is, our critical attention is drawn **inward**, to the subjective states that cannot be comprehended or expressed directly. My own preference, however, lies in a different direction. I do not want to discount the psychological reference that a myth might have, but I

Imagining: How Myths Are Made

would rather raise the pragmatic and epistemological question that turns our attention to the "real world" of experience, the world outside of the psyche, the world with which the psyche (or the "mind") interacts in its processes of comprehension. So, the "key" question that may spring the lock of myth is this: *What does the myth **imagine** by way of getting a hold on human experience?*

In this question, the verb is used with a certain "spin" on it. "To imagine" refers to a form of *bona fide* cognition, not to what the mind does in some idle or distracted mode. Think "to imagine" as, *mutatis mutandis*, "to know," "to understand." Part of the array of dictionary definition that one finds under "know" can be captured in "to imagine":

> "to apprehend with clarity or certainty"
> "to regard or accept as true beyond doubt"
> "to have a practical understanding of or thorough experience with"
> "to experience"
> "to have firmly secured in the mind or memory"
> "to be acquainted with or familiar with"

In order to appreciate the integrity of myth as an authentic way of knowing, I want to ask: What does the myth imagine? That is, what has the mythmaker "apprehended with clarity or certainty"? What does she regard or accept as true beyond doubt? What is it that she has experienced? What does she have firmly secured in mind or memory? When she tells or uses or refers to the myth, what can we discern as the "objects" with which she is acquainted or familiar?

That is, what does the mythmaker **know**? What "knowledge" does the myth convey, albeit in an "imaginative" manner? "To imagine" implies that the objects of sense experience, in their being "known," are transmogrified, into **image.** Hence the "knower" grasps the content of the "real world" quite literally **with** images. The mythmaker does not "conceptualize" experience. She pictures it, re-presents it, even to herself, as a facsimile or reflection or expression of the "thing itself." We might call it an "image," a dramatic rendition. The thing, ensconced in the mind, is "shadowed" by its own portrait--much as was Dorian Gray. His picture was "drawn forth from" him (that is the denotation of the Latin verb, *portrahere*) and took on a life of its own.

Religion and Mythology

We may not want to subscribe to this conceit without some reservation. Still, a portrait bears a complex relation to what is "represented" by it. It is not the thing itself; nor is it something else entirely. But I believe that we should allow as much ingenuity to the mythmaker as we do to any artist, that is to any one who skillfully represents some object in the real world outside or inside of her own **imagination.**

Over the centuries humans have invented or learned to use a great variety of cognitive modalities. I suspect that most of them fall along a continuum of mental operations that individuals learn in distinctive combinations and with habitual preferences. I want to argue, therefore, that the mythmaker's contribution to "knowledge" is by way of her **imagining** mountains, stars, rivers, heroes, events, social configurations, dreams, intimations--and even intuitions. The latter is a word also much abused. It derives from the Latin verb which simply means "to look toward or at, or to contemplate." An imaginative "looking" can yield a kind of knowledge that in its own right is valid and true.

Myth, then, is an artifact of one's imagining. That there may be better **explanations** of certain phenomena is no grounds for dismissing myths as inauthentic knowledge in their own right. "To imagine" means "to know" in a distinctive way. Our habits of cognition may have settled on other preferences over the last century and more. But there is evidence that just as we continue to fabricate plows and pots and engines and boats and houses--so we continue to fabricate myths as surrogates or substitutes or defaults for the kind of knowledge that we convince ourselves we prefer in this "age of science." But our preferences do not determine the possible range of validity. Myth represents a possible way of knowing that is still seductive and useful. Obviously! How strange, then, to consign all myth to the category of falsehood.

Myths are as much about the "real world" as they are effusions of the interior landscape. In fact, I am arguing, they provide an even larger window onto the world of ordinary experience when compared to the familiar revelations of the psyche. I do not want to deny, however, some degree of reciprocity between the two regions, but only to claim that myth has an integrity of its own as a way of knowing.

Imagining: How Myths Are Made

In a thousand ways, the following observation has been made: Everything one may observe about, let us say, the moon (or the Eiffel Tower or a grandparent or any object of experience) is equally an observation about oneself; and every observation about oneself (about behaviors, feelings or values) likewise reflects that object of experience. Myths, then, "negotiate" the boundaries between the Inside and the Outside. Ultimately, mythmaking dissolves the distance between these two worlds by powerful acts of the imagination.

Notes

1 From an advertisement for *The Scapegoat Generation* (Common Courage Press). Examples of this kind of usage are, of course, legion. Even though this particular example may not be the ultimate one, it should serve the purpose of the argument.

2 Richard Shenkman (New York: Harper & Row, 1988).

3 The etymology is surprisingly literal: *arte* is the case of "agent" of the Latin word for "skill." *Factum* means something that was made. Hence an "artifact" is an object "made with skill," that is, "crafted."

CHAPTER IV

MYTHMAKING AS A HABIT OF MIND : FAMILIARITY WHAT MAKES MYTHS POSSIBLE (AND NECESSARY)

Myths, then, are ghosts that haunt the houses of culture. They live in attics and basements. They wander into other inhabited parts of an estate where they rattle their bones and whistle in the night, or hide behind the curtains and in the closets during the day. Try as we might, we cannot ignore myths and, at the same time, we seem unable (even reluctant) to exorcise them. After all, many of us seem to harbor the suspicion that myths are still being created, even though we are sometime persuaded to call them lies. Some may even fancy that over the years even these presumptive lies may transmogrify into authentic antiques, *bona fide* artifacts that will eventually haunt the house of our future just as do those real ghost from some distant past.

If "imagining" is the "mechanism" that creates myth, are there any conditions necessary for that process to get under way? We have talked about imaginative cognition as though it were "just something that we did"; as though we could simply switch on our imagining and it would operate gracefully and spontaneously and predictably every time. I think not. We must look for the condition that sets our imagining to mythmaking.

I want to propose that it is **familiarity** with an object that provides such a condition. It is precisely familiarity that sets the stage for the imagination to shift into gear in preparation for "rendering experience intelligible in a dramatic mode." The very language of cognition contains an intimation of this proposition. An "archaic meaning" for the verb "to know" is "to have sexual intercourse with. . . ." Every innuendo of "familiarity" infuses this usage of "knowing." It implies that intimacy is a necessary condition for mythmaking.

Religion and Mythology

It must have been one of those folks that woke every day in the cottages on the lower slopes of Olympus that was able to convert this mountain into the home of the gods. The Ganges is mother to those who live and worship on its banks and bath often in its waters. Those devotees of Japanese Shinto who every day "bring up the Sun" at the top of Mount Fuji must surely "know" the volcano and the "Great-Sky-Shiner" intimately. Ceres depended on the familiarity of Greek farmers with their fields of grain; likewise *Kazahinomi-No-Miya* (the "wind deity"), who has a "home" not too far from the "Great-Sky-Shiner" at Ise Jingu, depended on the familiarity of devotees with the wind and weather for which they prayed.

A kind of existential awareness, perhaps a focused puzzlement in face of the human condition must lie behind the Mayan myths that accounted for the creation of mortals out of clay and then out of wood. For Native Americans to celebrate "Mother Earth" in story certainly requires a familiarity with the landscape as something "known" intimately over a life time and across the generations. A home can become a "mythic place" for the members of a family who have grown up there. We "know" the layout of our houses, even in the dark, after many months and years of finding our way around after the lights have been turned off for the night. A spouse turns into a virtual "mythic presence" after many years of cohabitation and conversation. Married persons come to know each other in ways that defy psychological analysis or even friendly explanation. Members of an athletic team develop a special intuitive knowledge of each other's "moves."

This kind of "knowledge" may have become suspect in an age driven by scientific research that puts a premium on "objectivity." But one wonders! Does not advanced research eventually depend on **intuition** as much as laboratory notes? May we not translate "intuition" as "intimacy"? May not sheer "familiarity" with a specimen or a process yield significant knowledge? Patriotism may some time be an aberrant form of this kind of knowing, especially if it moves people to insane defense of their "way of life." Or patriotism may be the twin of a nationalism that bestows upon an entire population a sense of identity that gives life its meaning.

I discovered an advertisement in a magazine that speaks to this "argument." On one side of the page is a photographic still life of a

Familiarity: What Makes Myths Possible

bowl of fruit and a bottle of wine on a table on a balcony overlooking the Adriatic Sea. Next to this picture--in a magazine of very recent vintage--is the text of the ad: We learn that Greece was "chosen by the Gods." The "argument" goes like this:

THE SPIRIT OF ZEUS LIVES ON

> Zeus, God of Gods. Father of mankind. Protector of strangers. In the land of the Gods, hospitality was a divine edict from none other than the God who ruled supreme on Mount Olympus.
>
> The spirit of Zeus lives on in this warm land. What the earth so generously provides, the Greeks share generously with strangers. "Filoxenia." A word that is uniquely Greek, describing a spirit that is uniquely Greek.
>
> Zeus invites you to Greece. To share the warmth of the Greek sun. To bask in the warm hospitality of the Greek people.
>
> Are the Greeks so friendly because of the Gods? Or, were the Gods taken with the friendliness of the Greeks? The Gods could have chosen any place on earth. They chose the warmth of Greece.

I grant that this exhortation to "Fly Olympic Airways" to Hellas may seem unworthy of serious discussion in a critical essay on mythmaking. But such a "come-on" has "mythic" overtones that seem to arise out of the kind of familiarity with a place that I have been talking about. Somewhere between the classical myth as specious contrivance or outmoded fantasy and myth as "taken for granted" by Homer, we find this not-so-naive panegyric of an ancient tradition. Suddenly, "the Gods" are real--or at least "real" enough to entice, for one imaginary moment, someone looking for a place to vacation. How **does** one, how **should** one deny that "the spirit of Zeus lives on"?[1] Is it possible that, absent of commercial motives, an "ancient people" were able to celebrate their virtues and their place, and to do so simply because of a spontaneous feeling of familiarity with the ambient world that they used to call Hellas?

Religion and Mythology

If we suppose that "knowing" is exclusively an abstractive process, then this proposition can hardly have much appeal. One cannot learn of traditional mythologies without realizing that there is one characteristic that brings them all under the same critical umbrella. They are stories, and stories are not abstractions. The mythmaker has turned intimacy and familiarity with objects of experience into **dramatic** representations. Is myth therefore art? I would argue that it is more like art than it is like science, though we should not underestimate the objectivity of knowledge that lies as a prior condition to mythic knowing.[2] But we must be cautious in forcing a casual alliance between art and myth.

In archaic societies, it seems, the aesthetic and the utilitarian qualities of art are not distinguished. Such "art" does not belong in museums, but remains embedded in a cultural context. It remains, quite literally, **vital**, still attached to the requirements of ordinary behavior. Appreciation is not detached from utility. Likewise with myth: it is not itself a **literary** artifact, though we often find myths conveyed into our time in epics or folktales. In this form, in which the content seems to have been embalmed by scribes and poets, the arrangement of the action and of the characters may be fashioned according to other canons than those that created the myths in the first place.

We should realize that myths only make sense in a setting in which vital issues of meaning and intelligibility, judging and deciding, ruling and officiating are at stake. Then the requirements of orderly plotting are not relevant. The content of the socially conditioned consciousness may come to the surface in a more random manner. The mythmaker gropes for intelligibility rather than devises entertainment for a patron. The stuff of immediate memory, the materials that are familiar and accessible to the imagination are the very stuff that myth is made of.

We might be closer to the "reality" of myth if we think of it as closer to street theater than to literary epic, more dependent on the logic of an oral recitation than it is the work of a *bona fide* novelist or playwright or poet contriving the residues of memory and observation in order to entertain or inspire an audience. Under such circumstances, myths are not exclusively aesthetic objects, devoid of psychological or

Familiarity: What Makes Myths Possible

social utility. They are the stories that people tell themselves and each other in order to stabilize their life boats.

Such stories may eventually be captured by persons who will routinize their use for the purposes of social or religious ritual. Sooner or later they will be recited on "official occasions" or will provide the raw materials of more formal entertainments.But, still, they began in the "imagining" of the real world where a compass was needed to negotiate the turbulence of life's rushing river. Eventually our life boats will be stabilized by conjuring out of memory the latent content of traditional stories that are more akin to dramatic vignettes than to creedal formulas or "scientific explanations." Such stories, I have argued, in their original moment "imagine" the "Outside," the world that orbits our consciousness and our conscience. But what more needs to be said about the "Outside"?

In even raising the issue in these terms, I suppose, I am still trying to fend off the influence of Joseph Campbell's reflections on mythmaking. There is no doubt that we do live in "the psychological society."[3] Campbell's approach to myths is a clear indication of this cultural habit, at least in the West. Under Campbell's tutelage, the rationalist's notion of myth as failed science is not even an issue. The "truth" of myth depends on its satisfying the needs of the psyche, of expressing the interior reality of spiritual heroes. It is as though human beings have always been primarily responsive to the movement of their interior tides. Andrei Codrescu, however, observes in "our time" what he calls "the disappearance of the Outside."[4]

His is a subtle argument to recreate. But, in my estimation, he puts forth an insight that throws important light on our current bias against myth as a legitimate way of knowing. Here is some of what he says in his critique of our time, as we face "the disappearance of the Outside":

> The Outside exists both in a physical, geographical dimension as parts of our planet yanked out of their specific ecology and made to turn about the petty tyranny of our desires, and in a metaphysical dimension, as an area accessible by religious feeling. In its physical sense it is the place where the human creature is equal to other living things, where it operates

ecologically in order to balance (create) the world, where it speaks with animals with or without shamans, where indeed it can forget itself. In its metaphysical sense it is the place of dreaming, accessible by imagination and poetry, where we have stubbornly insisted on going since we began as a species. This is the place of the original creative gesture, the apex of fertility where there is no difference between mind and matter. . . . That the two embodiments of the Outside [the geographical and the metaphysical] are disappearing together is the greatest tragedy that has befallen us so far, a tragedy much greater than an adverse history.[5]

I would argue that mythmaking was responsive unselfconsciously to "the Outside": to a full array of sensible experiences as well as to shared and solo insights into the human drama being played out on both the stages of society and nature and, indeed, on the stage of the cosmos. Myth was **about** the "experienced world," responsive at the same time to its incipient chaos and to the "rage for order" that seems to operate on the neurological level of the human organism. If that Outside has disappeared (or at least is being severely eroded or displaced) under the encroachment of a relatively new subjectivity or "interiority," then there is no wonder that we are suspicious of mythmaking. For that was a way of imagining experience that conjured a world, quite literally "in orbit" around the human selves that were restless and hopeful, anxious and serene, fully at home in the world and forever aliens. Codrescu comments on the opposite of "the Outside" in this way:

> As the interior becomes all there is, there is less and less to oppose to it. There is nothing to compare it to. The memory of the outside is also a form of interiority: the outside resides *in* memory. It can be argued that the interior is the space where everything disappears, including the bombardments of the media, that it is an active vacuum (or a series of vacuums, one inside another).[6]

It is clear that Codrescu's "analysis" is polemical. His insights still may have critical value for our attempt to understand how to get a critical hold on mythmaking. Think of culture as a repository, a great

Familiarity: What Makes Myths Possible

vault in which we accumulate what we no longer need on a daily basis but cannot casually discard. Codrescu is remembering the time when the human spirit was truly "objective," fascinated by a world that both sheltered and menaced it. Now the Inside and the Outside are separate domains, one assigned to psychologists and other to physicists and biologists. Both, however, laboring under the scientific habits of mind are obliged to produce theories of their respective worlds. Can we imagine a time when our "knowledge" was less divided, when "theorizing" had not yet been invented, when the mind imagined the Outside that intruded into its interior space and recited stories that reflected the encounter? Surely, there was a time when we lived on a two-way street, engaged in a reciprocal process with "reality." We then enjoyed a waltz of the spirit with the objects of experience, or a dance full of frenzy and hope, expressing the dark side of life.

My proposition is this: Human beings as creatures of community forget nothing! We have not forgotten how we made myths in that marvelous workshop of the psyche when the mind was in and of its world. Although we have been tempted to suppress that memory, it will not go away; it asserts itself even in the midst of our efforts to deny it. "Explaining" has not annulled imagining; theory has not erased drama. We will tolerate only so long the disparities and confusions that are inflicted on us by the ambient world. Even before we could decipher that world, we found ways of re-presenting it; even before we could resolve its enigmas, we captured them in the net of words and "plotted" our perceptions for the assurance of the mind that would not rest until it made some kind of sense of the incipient chaos that boils beneath the surface of appearances.

For many decades (even centuries), of course, the critical habit of mind has wanted to dismiss mythmaking as failed science or as simply an expression of the historical limitations of our knowledge. Eventually, the human race would completely outgrow the disposition to substitute fantasy for authentic knowledge. At least that seems to be the retrospective judgment. We are now in a position to appreciate what myth is and what it has been. There is no need any longer to belittle mythmaking for what it was not. It is foolish to repudiate those old habits of mind, especially when we realize that they in fact did a certain day's work--and are still fully eligible for employment. We need only appreciate the limits and the capabilities of myth.

We have changed our minds about the "disabled" among us. They are no longer to be defined by what they cannot do but by what they can do. Mythmakers are not and never were "scientists." A myth is not *ipso facto* any more a lie now than it ever was, though stories can be employed to deceive just as readily as theories and even hard data. *Myth is what myth does.* It is intellectually derelict to dismiss it for what it is not and for what it cannot do. There are many ways to deal with "the Outside," even if that has begun to fade in our consciousness. And even if it does appear to be fading, "the Outside" is still there, confronting even the mind that often prefers its own self-preoccupied embrace.

The psyche, whether focused on itself or on "the Other," still expresses a general preference for dramatic scenarios that promise some kind of solution while denying conclusions. That is, we are drawn to stories that create in us a degree of uncertainty and expectation. We wait for an intelligible outcome to actions and are fascinated by the ambiguity that surrounds them; we desire and resist resolutions of the mystery that envelopes imaginable events. So myths haunt not only the culture, but they also take up residence in the psyche, that array of intentional and unintentional operations that are at work in the vast cavern that we call our "minds."

Arising out of the duplicitous depths of that psyche, there are recurrent interests and strategies that are fundamental to mythmaking: heroic deeds, transitions from chaos to cosmos, visits to the underworld, origins of the world as a place for human life, the evolution of human consciousness and human form. There are surely many other "themes" that circulate through the imagination of mythmakers. Such stories themselves depend on a penchant for fantasy, that is, invented worlds embellished often with dream images or conscious visions. In any event, in order to make sense of myths we should discount the "failed science" interpretation and renounce the casual conviction that myths "explain the unexplainable."

As is often the case, when we are attentive to original usage, we can find in certain words a power that we often lose in casual employment. "To explain" quite literally means "to flatten out." Here

Familiarity: What Makes Myths Possible

is a clue to the difference between accounting scientifically for a phenomenon and imagining it. Surely imagining does not simplify the objects of experience. Myths do not "flatten out" what they imagine. On the contrary, mythmaking is more akin to elaboration or embellishment than it is to reduction or abstraction. That is why I argue that myths are not "scientific explanations" that have failed. They are what they do: myths render familiar experience intelligible in a dramatic mode and are themselves intelligible events of consciousness and sensibility.

We should now be in a position to lay out a plan for interpreting myths. Appropriate cautions have been indicated along the path that has brought us this far. Myths are not free-floating tales with no attachment to history or society. They are not casual entertainments nor spontaneous therapies generated merely to assuage our psyches. They are not in themselves literary in character, though they often provide the materials for literature. But we need to do more than elaborate what myths are **not**.

Our final task is the formal one of recommending a dialogical approach to myth. We must learn to appreciate mythmaking as an ancient habit of mind as well as a on-going process that may often embarrass and frustrate many in the twentieth century, though it continues to exhibit its dynamics in a world overwhelmed by information and baffled by ideologies. We must now try to refine the hermeneutic that has so far emerged as only a crude instrument for navigating the oceans spread out by the imagination.

Myths, as we have learned to think of them, come to us first of all as artifacts. It is as survivals from the past that we recognize those stories that often seem quaint and irrelevant. They are fashioned, as it were, with some tool, created with some instrument, on analogy with potter's wheels, hammers and levers. The tool that fashions myths, however, cannot be found among the material instruments used to shape and build the artifacts uncovered by archaeologists. We seek here for a more tenuous instrument, for a tool used by the mind.

The argument so far has insisted that it is a particular modality of cognition that creates myths. To realize what that instrument is we must learn how to use the verb "to imagine" on close analogy with the more common verb "to know." So mythmakers "imagine" mountains

Religion and Mythology

and rivers, heroic deeds and death, journeys and dreams, flora and fauna, and a thousand other "objects of experience." Ordinary "knowing" leaves residual abstractions in our minds; it deposits concepts or ideas, memory traces and faint longings, guesses and fantasies. But "imagining" gives us a different kind of recall and recognition. We realize this when we discover myth in the shadows of consciousness, or when we hear a story that retains perceptions and memories, or when we see with "the mind's eye" a dramatic rendition of a vision or an intuition. When the seer, the seen and the seeing converge in one moment of "knowledge," a myth has presented itself--or, if you prefer, the mind has conjured image and story out of the "evidences" of Aristotle's world. "Imagining," without fanfare of novelty, permits us "to know" what otherwise might baffle us or even pass unnoticed. It is a mode of cognition that is not suited to making or giving "explanations." It is a knowledge that does not "flatten out" the moments of encounter with objects of experience. Imagining creates fables; it makes narratives out of observations; it converts perceptions into vignettes; it renders metaphorical the ordinary, the dramatic and the mundane.[7] This way of knowing is more spontaneous than systematic. It finds its materials, as I have suggested, anywhere and everywhere. It confronts them across the entire range of "the Outside." It scavenges the empirical realm and responds, often unawares, to the motions of the interior landscape. Lévi-Strauss has characterized mythmaking as *bricolage*, the work of an ingenious handy-man who weaves memories and fantasies, facts and fictions, dreams and guesses into a narrative that corresponds to reality in the way many paintings "imitate" their subjects.

Such an enterprise of imagining is constrained by a purpose, an intention. Mythmakers "intend" the gods they conjure more than they "believe in" them. They express meaning as they see it in feeling states. Their purpose is "to purpose" an insight or suspicion. Their mission is to discern direction in events and to discover design in aleatory moments. Mythmakers are driven by some kind of necessity that is at least as much expressive of a personality as it is given by fate, though that is often the name by which it is called.

That necessity is discovered in the realm of experience; it is also invented as a way of reading "THE INELUCTABLE MODALITY OF

Familiarity: What Makes Myths Possible

THE VISIBLE."[8] Myth suspends us in a world in which what happens was inevitable and capricious at the same time. Or perhaps it was neither. But a story had to be told that would constrain the wind to drive the mill. A myth discovers agents in processes and recognizes the processes that capture agents: someone makes things happen and what happens reacts on those human agents of the "gods" who are willful pawns of fate. In short, the mythmaker sees into a world that is opaque and tells us what is there.

The effect of these fugues of the imagination is a definition of the world and of the distinctive creatures that inhabit it. Myth sets the limits of "the human" **and** delineates the boundaries of Earth and Sky. Myths also create narrative bridges between the two spheres of reality. In such stories, gods and heroes are, quite literally, "realized." They are conjured out of hopes and fears, brought into virtual existence to console the apprehensive and to encourage the hesitant. Life and death are presented to souls shipwrecked in a corner of the cosmos. And all that comes between being born and dying is anticipated and even celebrated before it happens so that retrospectively it was inevitable. Mythmakers meet us at the crossroads where Complexity and Simplicity lie in wait. They give their due to these two Tempters and warn us not to veer too close to this Scylla and Charybdis. They help us to see both the seduction and the satisfaction that either or both may bestow on human beings.

Mythmakers find in the world outside what they intuitively know about themselves, namely, that simplicity in the explanation or representation of any observable phenomena is counter-intuitive. Any presumptive notion of simplicity in the realm of our observations is clearly unconvincing. As human beings we have a deep irresistible preference for complexity. Being intricate organisms ourselves, we know that the world we inhabit reflects or shares in our intricacy. Or, to put it another way, as human beings we know (that is, we can "imagine") that we are complex entities and so **cannot** suppose that we are embedded in a non-complex reality. Any account that we contrive of this reality that surrounds us must, ironically, be appropriately complex. Hence, myths are not simple. That are not "Dick and Jane Stories" about Spot and Mommy and Daddy. Myths always develop in the direction of a level of complexity that baffles the person who must

Religion and Mythology

respond to them from outside the environment in which they were created.

In that environment, the mythic "plot" must, for at least two reasons, tend to complexity. First, the "plot" develops in a dynamic setting in which many persons contribute to its elaboration. These persons are embedded in a socio-historical structure that creates multiple perspectives that cry out for expression and many agenda that must be carried out. Hence, multiplicity of motives and interests work to elaborate the culture's mythology. The practical result are "plots,"[9] that is, mythic scenarios, that are convincing if they are appropriately intricate.

Second, since the "plot" develops under the impulse of the active imagination, it is never closed or finished. The plot takes on a life of its own. One can always imagine another twist or turn in the mythic action or some "development" in the mythic characters. Since the mythic scenarios have been "imagined" in the first place, there are no natural limits to the complexity that they can exhibit. How could the imagination define its own boundaries? Quite literally, "the sky is the limit." If we change the metaphor, we may say that the imagination always finds itself gazing into a bottomless well, trying to see into a darkness that grows deeper the farther we push our looking. What is there either in the well or in our imagination that defines their fixed limits? *Nothing.*

Scientific inquiry knows when and where to stop before it changes direction or picks up where it left off. But, however far scientific inquiry does proceed, it is always responsive to the imperative, "Do not multiply entities." That is, legitimate theorizing does not make explanations more complicated than they need to be. Simplification is the rule of scientific inquiry. Not so in mythmaking. In that kind of cogitation, complexity is both natural and necessary. By definition and by intuitive sensibility, imagination can impose no restraints on itself. On the contrary: It is in the very nature of the imagination that it should reflect complexity rather than insist on simplification.

Hence, scientific inquiry and mythmaking are divergent paths to understanding. Along the one path, one disciplines herself to "explain" phenomena; along the other, one indulges herself in the "representation" of human experience. Which path leads to "Truth"? Since such a

Familiarity: What Makes Myths Possible

question begs a host of other philosophical questions, perhaps we should avoid it.[10] We have for centuries, however, been learning a bias that favors the "explanatory" path to knowledge, yet we still seem unable to shake off the penchant to "re-present" the world of our experience--and to do so in ways consistent with our intuitive awareness that nothing as intricate as human beings could ever be satisfied with the simplifications of rational knowledge that tend to "flatten out" our responses to experience.

And so myth always tends toward complexity rather than simplicity. Eventually, the outsider loses her way in an effort to "follow" such plots. Then we respond to our own frustration as "outsiders" by belittling these creations of the human imagination, these rhetorical fugues that could in principle go on forever, never reaching a fixed limit in the non-explanatory dramatizations that we call "myths." Then, ironically, and against our very nature, we presume to dismiss such stories as objects of intellectual disdain, berating them for what they never could be and then casting them as falsehoods before even venturing into dialogue with them. But just as conscience forbids us from casually discarding other kinds of artifacts, so habits of mind are not so easily broken.

In a provocative political commentary published in 1992, William Greider finds himself tempted by the ancient resonance of myth. He says,

> In the age of mass media, the president [of the United States] is shielded from scrutiny by qualities that other politicians cannot claim--the *mythic powers* of his office and his ability to broadcast the largest and most deceptive messages of all.[11]

Why "mythic" powers? Why "powers"? Gilgamesh and Agamemnon, Zeus and Rudra and Odin--these and other mythic heroes and gods, stalk the labyrinth of Greider's imagination as he tries to bring into focus the current political scene. He need not analyze the content or method of that power, because, for a metaphoric moment, he allows himself "to imagine" it. In the almost casual adjective, "mythic," the author strikes a chord in our imagination. We see what he sees and hear what he hears: There is available to presidents a "power" whose dimensions cannot be mapped and whose use cannot be easily predicted. The extraordinary complexity of "presidential power" is evoked by the not-so-simple adjective, "mythic." Surely myth deserves this kind of respect and attention. It begs us to speak with it about what it imagines.

Intellectual courtesy and historical sensitivity, then, require us to respect the stories that arise out of the myriad encounters with the familiarities of the natural and historical worlds of experience. The artifacts are still functional and, in fact, can help us speak about things too familiar for mere words and discursive sentences. If we allow mythmakers, both those in our past and those still recreating our memories and hopes, to **imagine** the **familiarities** of experience, we may lose a certain precision of knowledge that is possible in explanations. However, the gains in affective insight into human experience of "the world" should be--indeed, has been--worth the sacrifice.

Notes

1 We should recall here Berger's observation that myth "cannot be disconfirmed by empirical evidence in the minds of its adherents." (See above.)

2 See Shirley Park Lowry, *Familiar Mysteries, The Truth in Myth* (New York: Oxford University Press, 1982). Though I do not always agree with Lowry's approach to interpreting myths, her recognition that myth employs the data of every-day experience is part of an argument seldom made with such clarity.

3 *The Psychological Society* is the title of a very provocative book by Martin L. Gross (New York: Simon and Schuster, 1978). The author issues what I take to be an implicit warning about the hazards posed by that "psychological society": "Much has been said about the awesome *external* transformation in our modern world. These changes are obvious. But the *internal* shift in man's psyche has altered both our actions and expectations more than any technological force. This change in inner man has taken place quietly, yet it has altered the nature of our civilization beyond recognition." (p. 3.)

Familiarity: What Makes Myths Possible

4   See Andrei Codrescu, *The Disappearance of the Outside: A Manifesto for Escape* (Massachusetts: Addison-Wesley, 1990)

5   Codrescu, pp. 200-201.

6   Codrescu, p. 198.

7   For a fascinating discussion of the power and use of metaphor in both language and thought, see *Metaphors We Live By* by George Lakoff and Mark Johnson (Chicago and London: University of Chicago Press, 1980). In a critical note about this book, we learn that the authors understand that "Reality itself is defined by metaphor, and as metaphors vary from culture to culture, so do the realities they define." In a final statement, the authors offer the following judgment that is consistent with the argument that I have developed in this chapter and throughout: "It is as though the ability to comprehend experience through metaphor were a sense, like seeing or touching or hearing, with metaphors providing the only ways to perceive and experience much of the world. Metaphor is as much a part of our functioning as our sense of touch, and as precious." (p. 239) It is not inappropriate for my purposes to paraphrase that last sentence as follows: *Imagining* is as much a part of our functioning as any other sensible or cognitive strategy, and as indispensable to our relentless effort to make sense of a complex and elusive array of experience available to us as human beings.

8   James Joyce, *Ulysses* (New York: The Modern Library, 1946), p. 88.

9   We should note here that *mythos* is the term used by Aristotle in his *Poetics* to designate the actual **plot** of the tragic dramas that he analyzes in this work of literary criticism.

10 For an interesting support of this strategy, see *Consequences of Pragmatism* by Richard Rorty (Minneapolis: University of Minnesota Press, 1982), especially "Introduction: Pragmatism and Philosophy," pp. xiii-xvii.

11 William Greider, *Who Will Tell The People* (New York: Simon and Schuster, 1992), p. 143.

CHAPTER V

CODA TO PART II

Robert Pirsig, in his book *Lila*,[1] finds an insight that may help us realize that it is possible to be done with an inquiry without completing it. When I began the reflections that I have laid out so far in this book, I felt an apprehension not unlike what one feels before leaving home on a journey that is not fully arranged or predictable. Then, as I saw the end in sight, I grew worried about actually finishing the essay. I was puzzled by that apprehension. Why not a sense of relief such as one might feel when arriving home, having gone around the world in eighty days?

At the moment I reached the last page of Pirsig's book, I understood the worry that nagged me. The finale to his "inquiry into morals," his rounding off his "Metaphysics of Quality," seemed for a split second terribly anticlimactic:

> Good is a noun. That was *it*. That was what Phædrus had been looking for. That was the homer, over the fence, that ended the ball game. Good as a noun rather than as an adjective is all the Metaphysics of Quality is about. Of course, the ultimate Quality isn't a noun or an adjective, or anything else definable, but if you had to reduce the whole Metaphysics of Quality to a single sentence, that would be it.[2]

At first, "That was *it*" seemed inconsistent with the open, sometimes groping way that Pirsig pursued his intellectual obsession. Then, when I thought that one should give any author the benefit of a doubt, I realized that there was an odd virtue embedded in that concluding paragraph. What seemed to be the end of the road, was in fact the beginning of a new personal and intellectual journey.

Upon reflection I realized that the statement that "Good is a noun," opens a gate onto farther roads along which thought can travel. Pirsig's conclusion has the virtue of being inconclusive. It does not provide a key that one can use to lock the gate of inquiry and establish a secure fortress of dogmatic certainty. Pirsig does not offer the reader a refuge from the authentic confusion of a "dynamic" (Pirsig's word) vision of what the human mind and heart are capable of. Instead, he validates the penchant for puzzles that drives so much of human thought.

I was worried that my thoughts on religious experience and mythmaking might come across as dogmatic and that they would not be as intelligible to others as they were to me. After all, one can always believe he is making sense when one is talking to oneself. So, having been momentarily deceived by Pirsig's "last word," I worried that my essays might appear to actual readers to be a *fait accompli*, terminal thoughts rather than points of departure.

In fact, however, I had neither hoped nor planned to make definitive sense of behaviors as complex as mythmaking, as elusive as religious experience. So what haunts me now is the suspicion that a reader might actually "believe" what I have said. Because those thoughts have been inscribed "in black and white," the reader could take this argument as evidence of an overbearing personal confidence that my last thoughts mark a final destination. Many others who have thought about religion and myth have left me with just that impression. That was the burden of the chapter, "Mythmaking as a Habit of Mind: Circumspection."

Having followed Pirsig to his "conclusion" ("Good is a noun," and so forth), my own philosophical reflections changed backwards and forwards. Having proposed, almost casually, though in a breathless moment, that the best approach to understanding religious experience was to doubt the validity of the "belief paradigm," I then proposed to replace it with the critical notion of "experienced relationships." Then I went on to argue that to understand mythmaking we should enter into a dialogue with the process and its agents, and to observe the persistent marriage of religious experience to mythmaking over the millennia. When we actually entered the realm of mythmaking, I trust that the reader felt a gate opening rather than closing. How else to retain one's intellectual virtue in the presence of a habit of mind that takes us back to a time before "rational knowledge" and holds promise for clarifying our own thoughts in an unsettled present? Perhaps I should have developed the idea of "dialogue" more fully; perhaps I should have elaborated some of the other thoughts that I have assembled in this essay. Perhaps! But any self-respecting "essay" is an **attempt** at

Coda to Part II

hitting a moving target, a **venture** into a domain clouded by time and the ordinary limits of human understanding. Montaigne set the rule, in the sixteenth century, that "essays" are, quite literally, attempts at testing a subject. I hope that I have not broken that time-honored rule.

Although neither Agamemnon nor Odysseus were engaged in an intellectual enterprise, the latter is surely a more likely hero than the former in a philosophical quest that celebrates the marriage of religion and myth. When Agamemnon returned home he became the victim of his own intractable arrogance. Odysseus, on the other hand, returned home after incredible adventures, and then, having settled his affairs, took an oar on his shoulder and moved on to unknown territories. He was commanded by his guardian deity eventually to plant his oar in the ground and expect the natives to mistake it for a flail. Especially for inquiries of this sort, that strikes me as the right attitude. I trust, however, that the reader will not, as did those who met the restless Odysseus, mistake my oar for a flail. If so far my oar has pulled us through the ocean of religion, the next stage of this voyage of exploration will take us into the actual territory of mythology with an eye to finding still other clues to the apparent mysteries of these cultural artifacts. Before we have finished, we shall have experimented with other ideas that may help us to figure out "how myths are made" and "what makes myths possible."

In the final stage of this quest for understanding, I shall first try to see myths as stories that put history in the service of "Truth." Mythmakers convert events into dramatic scenarios that inspire and reassure those willing to listen with a sense of their exceptional origin and destiny. That is, (hi)story makes sense despite its likely appearance, to some, as "just one damn thing after another." Next I shall argue that myths also "reveal" the alternative visions that drive the many revelators that come to life in the sagas of historic religions. In the service of religious traditions, mythmakers have conjured for religious folks visions of "what is really going on" behind the ordinary facade of nature or history. And, finally, I shall try to show that mythmaking is still at work in shaping our perceptions of the world we live in. This "habit of mind" continues to "imagine" the world and to create "surrogate myths" that interpret a full range of possible--and impossible--experience. Now as then, not all mythmaking is dedicated to the articulation of *bona fide* religious experience. Its applications may be more varied than that. But in the storytelling that imagines the familiarities of this world and dramatically conjures those subtle relationships that sustain and move human beings and communities, myth is still married to religion.

Notes

1 Robert M. Pirsig, *Lila, An Inquiry into Morals* (New York: Bantam Books, 1991).

2 Pirsig, p. 409.

PART III

MYTHOLOGY IN THE SERVICE OF RELIGION

CHAPTER I

HISTORY IMAGINED AS TRUTH

The marriage contract between religion and myth puts a special burden on the latter. The mythmaking imagination must convert history into dramatic story in order to preserve a community's connections to its origin and to its destiny. Religious traditions will mine the historical memory of witnesses and victims of events so that they can serve the Truth at their foundations. Such Truth may arise from the insight of some great personality or, presumably, from a source ensconced in the heavens or beyond. It may be rooted in popular wisdom or prophetic intuition; it may be a subtle inference from long and deliberate observation of natural or historical processes or events. One way or the other, the imagination, in the service of religious experience, will transpose what it sees into a mythic mode.

The Durant's in a "postlude" to their ten volume *The Story of Civilization*, refer to the "troublesome duplexity" of history. They find a place in both apartments of the duplex by defining history "as the events or record of the past."[1] The conjunction "or," of course, disqualifies their comment as having much critical value in the complicated philosophical debate over the nature of history. Still, their unabashed desire to find "the lessons of history" may give us some clue in our present effort to understand what history is and what it does for religious traditions. The Durant's tell the reader what their labors have accomplished: The story of civilization tells us "what history has to say about the nature, conduct and prospects of man."[2]

Religion and Mythology

At least in retrospect, it is clear to Will and Ariel Durant that "history" is a teacher, or better an accounting of the past that reveals the future. But that forced optimism is tempered with a final humanistic gesture. On the last page of their "postlude" they confess that "the historian will not mourn because he can see no meaning in human existence except that which man puts into it. . . ."[3] Religious history, of course, is not so modest. It would deny, if not denounce, the presumption that it is "our pride that we ourselves may put meaning in our lives, and sometime a significance that transcends death."[4] The history **generated by** religious traditions, both formally and casually, either by revelation or insight, exhibits a very different perspective.

Almost always, from a tradition's bias, what happened is prologue to an unfolding story of creation, redemption, consolidation of power, or penetration of the cosmic mystery. The past, in which "great events" transpired, somehow determines the present and the future portrayed in the mythical tales that justify religious traditions. All was preparation, "once upon a time," for what "has now come to pass." Myths, quite precisely, *imagine* the past so as to validate the subsequent claims made by adherents of a particular tradition.

An example of this pattern is in the panegyric of Shoghi Effendi in his foreword to the history of the Baha'i Faith. The title of this "record of the past" is auspicious indeed and makes the same point as the narrative itself. In *God Passes By*, Effendi looks backward to find out what events "have to say" about our recent, our present and our future reality:

> Already in the space of less than a century the operation of the mysterious processes generated by [the Baha'I Faith's] creative spirit has provoked a tumult in human society such as no mind can fathom. Itself undergoing a period of incubation during its primitive age, it has, through the emergence of its slowly-crystallizing system, induced a fermentation in the general life of mankind designed to shake the very foundations of a disordered society, to purify its lifeblood, to reorientate and reconstruct its institutions, and shape its final destiny.[5]

Shoghi Effendi was the nephew of Abdul Baha, the son of Baha'u'llah, the founding revelator of the Baha'i Faith. Given that

History Imagined as Truth

"dynastic" connection and the "missionary" intent of the book, it seems fair to consider it an example of the species "religious history." *God Passes By*, then seems to me a clear example of "history in the service of 'truth'" and, hence, history transposed into a "mythic mode." The rhetoric in this passage (and in the entire book) is extraordinary. Words, phrases and sentence structure conspire to turn recollection into hope, events into processes, historical moments into mythic scenarios.

Here one finds no critical agonies over the academic questions about history. Effendi never once pauses to consider whether history is event or record. Nor does he falter in the presence of the great question, "Is history, as narrative, an objective science?" Even for our purposes, such arcane issues need not distract us. By this decision we set aside the theological problem of "historicity" and the metaphysical question of the nature of the divine reality. We seek only to understand what kinds of things go on in religious traditions--how they define themselves, how they present themselves.

W. H. Walsh's claim seems self-evident:

> The presence and operation of judgments of intrinsic importance in history seem hard to deny, and if this is correct the doctrine of fully scientific history must go by the board, for clearly enough you cannot read such judgments out of the facts.[6]

Histories generated by religious traditions are clear cases in point. They are repositories and conveyors of such judgments and hence can lay no claim to being "fully scientific." If we should ever want to compare a religious version of events (replete with appropriate judgments!) with some other version, the best that would be available is "consensus history." Even that, of course, would be a record of events that could lay no claim to "scientific objectivity." Walsh, again, in his deliberate way of thinking about the "limits of scientific history" helps us to grasp what is possible for the historical enterprise:

> There is, first of all, the fact that the historian (for example) of the French Revolution is a man who has a story to tell, that he is himself a particular person telling it and that he necessarily does his work with at any rate a general kind of audience in mind. The way someone tells a story depends not merely on what he has to

tell; it depends also, in respects with which we are all familiar, on
his own interests and preconceptions and those of the persons for
whose benefit he is telling it. This does not mean that stories are
irretrievably biased; it means only that every story contains an
account of the facts as seen from a particular point of view. There
is, if we like to use a dangerous term, a subjective component to
every story, or to put the point less misleadingly, every narrative
is someone's narrative, told, we may add, to some other party. To
treat a narrative without reference to narrator or audience is to
leave something of real importance out of account.[7]

What is true, then, of any history, is also true *a fortiori* of religious history "in the service of Truth."

The strictures of theological history are also observed by Patrick Burke. He argues that "the conceptual and logical basis of any religion is always our interpretation of our personal experience."[8] That claim somehow persuades him that it is not justifiable to base a religion on a historical event, as do the traditions of Semitic origin. He clinches his judgment with the rationally indisputable statement that "there cannot be adequate grounds for ascribing a specially divine origin to one event rather than another."[9] But what are "adequate grounds" for persons held hostage by their own personal experience, if not that personal experience itself, even when embedded in a historical community? Indeed, it seems impossible to expunge the marks of "personal experience" from any human creation, from statues to epics, from governments to murals to pious proverbs. And since religions, from our point of view, qualify as human creations, we need not despair if they bear such marks.

Burke's argument, however, is at least disputable. The justifiability of founding religious traditions on historical events is quite irrelevant in face of the fact that billions of people over many centuries have been engaged by such interpretations of events. Besides, other interpretive strategies than those based strictly on "personal experience" have been worked out to account for events on the landscapes of nature and the human psyche as well as on the stage of history.

There may be all sorts of assumptions reverberating in such strategies, depending on doctrinal formulations, beliefs, and even attitudinal biases. But is there any religious tradition that does not commit what Burke considers a logical mistake? Is there any religious tradition that does not envision or "re-vision" some part of its own past or, even more grandly, the universal history of humankind? To be religious means to appropriate a particular or particularized past, a past that may be represented with its temporal boundaries obscured, a historical past in which there are dynamics at work that may do extreme violence to common sense or even to certain knowledge. But no self-respecting religion can act as though it were free-floating in the ocean of historic time. Any tradition will gather together events, real or imaginary, into a coherent story that either justifies its conventional claims or renders its truth intelligible in a large, possibly cosmic framework.

Let us call the history created by specific religious traditions "special history." By examining examples of special histories, we may be able to generalize about the strategies for converting facts or alleged facts into the (hi)story[10] that particular traditions present both to their followers and to the world outside the tradition. There is no implication, however, that persons will have intentionally and deceitfully fabricated the (hi)story merely for political or polemical purposes. If such special histories are in fact misconstructions, they are that under the legitimate impulse to **interpret** events and experience. And even if some misconstructions had been intentional or deceitful, the tradition cannot be held accountable. Even the person who had created the special history from what may, in retrospect, be considered questionable motives was almost certainly acting under the imperative of a higher authority or of a severe personal persuasion.

The creators of special histories, then, were not liars, even if they fabricated the (hi)story that subsequently became canonical. Or at least we will never be able to support the judgment that they were, on the basis of evidence acceptable in a court of objective inquiry. Special histories, then, should be considered, in a neutral sense of the term, "propaganda"; that is, events that "ought to be propagated." The logic of "ought" may vary from tradition to tradition, but the imperative is felt in good faith by those who respond to it. The "priceless moment" on which the imperative is founded may be obscured for us in our present time. But certainly we should be prepared to appreciate any impulse or experience that made the creation of a special history as irresistible as the rising of any ocean tide.

But even if some special history could be shown to have originated through deceitful contrivance, once the construct has been accepted in a tradition, it is sure to be defended as authentic and valid. If anyone doubts its veracity, ingenious justifications can be devised to dampen criticism. Christian scholars and polemicists have over the last 200 years joined battle over the verifiability of Biblical history or even more often conspired to save Biblical history from the death of a thousand qualifications. Other traditions have also had to shore up their special histories to protect them from the erosive affects of modern empiricism. Our examination, however, will neither attack nor defend special histories. We will be satisfied to discern the peculiar characteristics of such (hi)stories that make them different from "consensus histories." Certainly one of the most elaborate examples of special history is that on which the Church of Jesus Christ of Latter-day Saints basis its religious claims.

First of all, no part of Mormon special history is construed, preserved, or represented merely to satisfy curiosity. That Church's history is (hi)story in the service of truth.

The history of the Church in general and the history in *The Book of Mormon* in particular have long been the center of a stormy controversy. Some have expressed doubts about the factual validity of the "American Scriptures"; others have reconstructed institutional history to make the Mormon movement seem less than virtuous. Other traditions, of course, have had their special histories questioned. The Mormons, however, have used the attacks as occasions for reaffirming the validity of their historical claims. The clearest example of this strategy is found in the two volume work, *A New Witness for Christ in America*. In the first volume there is a "Foreword" that reveals the defensiveness of the Church in the face of conventional historical criticism. Referring to *The Book of Mormon*, Eldin Ricks says: "But wisely or otherwise, many people are unwilling to consider seriously the credibility of the new witness's (i.e., *The Book of Mormon*'s) testimony about Christ's origin until certain questions about the books' own origin have been satisfactorily resolved."[11] The two volumes constitute the Church's response to this dilemma.

History Imagined as Truth

The descriptive subtitles of the two volumes indicated clearly that the work is part of the apologetics of the Church of Latter-day Saint. In the first volume, the reader learns that the book presents "Evidence of Divine Power in the 'Coming Forth' of The *Book of Mormon*." In the second, we find "Attempts to Prove *The Book of Mormon* Man-Made Analyzed and Answered." Both volumes, then, are concerned to demonstrate that the "American Scriptures" are both historically accurate and of non-human origin. *The Book of Mormon* is for the Church a special history that is true (factual) and serves the Truth (doctrinal validity). From within a tradition, especially one emerging from Biblical religion, one would expect an insistence on such a correspondence. But certainly the "facts" must undergo some change when mustered to serve the Truth. What, then, makes a history "special"? The question can be answered with reference to the techniques as well as the aims or the effects of the special history.

Again, we shall focus on the Mormons as providing an exemplary case. Their special history exhibits quite explicitly what must be inferred in the case of many other traditions, i.e., the truth of the record depends on its origin. Its factual validity is guaranteed by the character of the agent who recorded it, "an angel of light," himself a participant observer in an exceptional drama. A series of events that is continuous with and divergent from the same history that is preserved in the Hebrew and Greek Bible is faithfully recorded by the angel. The practical effect of this series of events has been the founding of a Christian Church that did not suffer the acculturation of the Church in Europe nor its sectarian fragmentation.

The Mormon special history reveals the once hidden scenario of the Church waiting to be re-established in the nineteenth century. There is no necessity to undertake the futile labor of **reforming** a Church already hopelessly contaminated by earlier reformations. The (hi)story makes it clear and certain: By virtue of a historical miracle the true Church can be reestablished in these "latter-days," the Church that by divine foresight and predetermination had been saved in chrysalis after a long preparation that tied it closely with the same Biblical history that had eventuated in the Catholic Churches.

Many of the Saints were persuaded to put their own reputation on the line to affirm that this special history was no fabrication. In *The

Religion and Mythology

Book of Mormon itself, one finds the following assurance to the faithful:

> "And we declare with words of soberness, that an angel of God came down from heaven, and he brought and laid before our eyes, that we beheld and saw the plates, and the engravings thereon; and we know that it is by the grace of God the Father, and our Lord Jesus Christ, that we beheld and bear record that these things are true."[12]

In later years, another, more mundane verification has been undertaken to prove that the special history is no fantasy of an overwrought soul. Archeological research is being brought to bear in support of the special history. Even in current editions of *The Book of Mormon*, there are colored photographs of artifacts clearly meant to suggest a connection between the canonical history and some actual course of events. The Church has issued films and pamphlets that also point to such a connection. The implication is clear: The revealed history corresponds to empirical history; the sacred record is factually verifiable. But how could it be otherwise--within the Tradition? It is unthinkable that God would be mocked by the facts; it is impossible that events would not follow a course corresponding to the divine plan. These are the certainties that underlie the special history of the Church of Latter-day Saints.

Is it possible to observe this Mormon history in order to discern the techniques of its construction, the aims and effects of its propagation and the assumptions underlying it? If so, then we may have found an approach to one tradition that may help our comprehension of other traditions. If we can understand how crucial events are **mythologized** by the Mormons, we may have found an approach to religious traditions that not only clarifies that Church's self representation but also reveals a process that is characteristic of all religious traditions, insofar as they are human phenomena.

What is it, then, that makes Mormon history special? Something happens to facts (whether real or alleged) in the canonical history that raises them above conventional requirements of verification. It is true, of course, that the Church currently argues that "the Archaeology and

History Imagined as Truth

Ethnology of the western continent contribute some corroborative evidence in support of *The Book of Mormon*."[13] But such efforts to establish the "historicity" of the saga of *The Book of Mormon* are not relevant to the question as I have put it. Even if the facts were verified, the crucial question would remain: What happens to the facts so as to produce a "special history"? All traditions that claim Semitic parentage have been drawn into the dilemma created by the rage for empiricism that emerged the eighteenth century. The revealed truth needs also to be checked against humanistic research. But that is a requirement that does not come naturally to religious traditions. Rather it is an apologetic strategy, a defensive tactic that cooperates with an "enemy" that raised the question of the objectivity of "scripture" to large proportions in the nineteenth century.[14]

Our concern, however, is with the creation of the special history, not with its defense. It is clear what happens, in the Mormon instance, to the alleged historical data. In order to see clearly the elementary process that makes a historical series special, we must, of course, set aside the critical requirement of factual verification. *The Book of Mormon*, as it comes to us, is a history analogous to that recounted in the Hebrew Bible, both in style and substance. To live within the tradition requires a willing suspension of disbelief with regard to the prehistoric events. Our question is, what renders that alleged history special?

What happens to the supposed facts in the Hebrew Bible happens also to the alleged facts in *The Book of Mormon*. They are transposed into a mythic mode and set in a context that makes them continuous with a historical process of cosmic proportions. What happens in the Ancient Near East and eventually in the Americas is not parochial drama. All events extraneous to this grand sequence are filtered out. The rest of human history is neglected because in the careers of Lehi, his ancestors and his successors, a drama is being played out that is under the direction of the Lord of Creation.

Appropriately, then, the (hi)story of *The Book of Mormon* is highly stylized, exhibiting an awed respect for the actors, both those on the stage and the One clearly at work behind the scenes. In the historical litany, what happened is what "came to pass," as though all events were standing in line waiting their turn. Nothing occurs that is gratuitous.

Religion and Mythology

Like a slow rumble of drums, a purpose vibrates through the (hi)story, at first almost inaudibly, gradually increasing in volume until the crescendo reaches a climax that lies outside the canonical narrative, though continuous with it. The record is revealed to Joseph Smith, and that record provides the basis for re-establishing a Church in America whose authority has not been compromised by pagan influences, political seductions or philosophical irrelevancies.

Alleged facts have been transposed into a mythic mode. The special history is formal, repetitive, and often incredible. It consists in a record of events that is, as Peter Munz would explain, "embroidered and organized for the sake of emphasis and clarity."[15] In this case, the alleged events, though much effort is made to certify them by research as well as by inspired testimony, are "pried loose" from their "position in space and time."[16] A serial event is thereby deprived of its status as a particular event and made to carry "a meaning over and above the meaning the particular event had at the time and place at which it occurred."[17] In Joseph Smith's imagination, "history" was represented as myth, and in the life of the Church that myth is subsequently accepted as history--albeit, from our critical point of view, a special history.

In general terms, what is the effect of transposing history into a mythic mode? It is to establish a revelatory basis for all other certainties of the Church. The details that create the appearance of verisimilitude in the special history are only incidental to the larger theme: Throughout the dim past, a divine plan has been working, otherwise unknown except for its inspired preservation by an angel of light. By various stylistic, personal and institutional strategms, the medium in which the preservation is realized emerges as an authoritative reference book for the Church. Its veracity is unimpeachable. The book reveals a past that justifies the present and the future. That it may be a fiction is irrelevant. Transposed into a mythic mode, the particular history is universalized. The special history reverberates with the sound of an authority so persistent that no one drawn into its echo chamber can doubt that she is hearing the divine rhapsody, celebrating a cosmic fulfillment.

The assumption, if we can credit devotional convictions with such a formal status, is that history has been revealed in the service of Truth.

History Imagined as Truth

A veil has been removed so that those whose sight had been obscured by mortal confusion can now see clearly what has been going on. Having dutifully suffered through the night, the Saints have seen a light break over them that was long eclipsed by savage neglect. The assumption, the unexpressed and inexpressible conviction at work here, is that the universe is so constituted that veils must be dramatically removed before the denizens of earth can see serial history in complex phase with cosmic history.

The human imagination, then, creates a species of history that serves not only to interpret personal experience but also to authenticate institutional claims. It is, of course, divine revelation or inspired insight that the religious tradition insists creates the special history. That revelation or insight may be the reciprocal of the human imagination, but a tradition is not likely to acknowledge such an association, since "imagination" is often felt as the creator of fantasies or even illusions. Still, it is by trying to find one's way between those particular antinomies of imagination and revelation that one may find a road of approach not only to the Mormon tradition, but to other traditions as well. The impulse to transpose "history" into a mythic mode is demonstrable in canonical and often in certain non-canonical histories. For even in more objective renditions of Mormon history one finds the same urge to justify the Church by romantic or idealizing enlargement of the historical context. So, here and in other historic religious movements, one discerns the process by which history is specialized; that is, one witnesses history created or re-created in the service of Truth.

Ahmadiyyat is a modern sect of Islam. In 1889, Mirze Ghulam Ahmad declared that he was the Mahdi promised in the traditions of the Prophet, Christ returned, Krisna realized, as well as the fulfillment of Zoroastrian and Buddhist "prophecies." The movement, that presents itself as the renaissance of Islam, has its center in Rabwah, Pakistan and carries on extensive missionary work in Africa, Asia and America. Not only has Ahmadiyya Islam developed a special historical account of the life of "the Promised Messiah," it has also reconstructed the (hi)story of Jesus. That special history transposes a large array of Biblical, local and other histories into polemical narratives.

Religion and Mythology

In bare outline, this phase of Ahmadi special history portrays Jesus as having been "saved from the accursed death on the cross." The negative side of this historical claim is that Jesus did not go "alive to the heavens" after his crucifixion but rather, when he had recovered from a trauma-induced swoon, was able to travel "through many countries east of Palestine and [then] spent the rest of his life in his final destination, Kashmir, where his tomb can still be seen today."[18] It can be found on Khanya Street in Srinagar.

This (hi)story is elaborately worked out by several Ahmadi Muslims, but all versions depend on the argument set forth in 1899, in the book *Jesus in India* by Hazrat Ahmad of Qadian, the Madhi/Messiah and founder of the Movement.[19] The book adduces "proofs from established facts" that are gleaned from the Bible, the Qur'an, and other Islamic texts, as well as from Buddhist, Hindu, medical and historical texts many of which are not "sacred." This special history of Jesus has two uses for Ahmadi Muslims.

First, there is the "internal" use to

> remove the serious misconceptions which are current among Muslims and among most Christian sects regarding the earlier and the later life of Jesus (on whom be peace);--misconceptions, the dangerous implications of which have not only injured and destroyed the conception of Divine Unity, but the unwholesome and poisonous influence of which has for long been noticed in the morals of the Muslims of this country.[20]

Ahmad goes on: "Spiritual maladies, i.e. want of good morals, evil thoughts, callousness, want of sympathy, are spreading among most Islamic sects, being the result of beliefs in unfounded stories and anecdotes of this kind."[21] The special history, then, should have a theological and therefore a moral effect on the followers of Ahmad, the Promised Messiah, whose mission is to restore to Islam the logical purity of its beliefs and its original passion for universality.

This special history, from the very beginning, has moved Ahmadi Muslims to confront and challenge other traditions. The Movement regularly issues scholarly and logical rebuttal of the orthodox Christian claim about Jesus' life "after death." The polemical intent is clear--to

History Imagined as Truth

establish the Ahmadiyya Movement as the fulfillment of the prophecies of all the world's viable religions and especially to set straight the story of Jesus' crucifixion.

What can one say about this special history? In a manner very like that of the Mormons, history has been reconstructed, transposed into a mythic mode that haunts the mind with esoteric truths. This special version of Jesus' career lets one in on secrets that should have been known, 'lo, these many years. One can master this version and learn to recite the events in the serial tale and to deduce the theological and moral implications that are significant in establishing the identity of a follower of the Promised Messiah. The special history has a mythic ring and as such represents a coherent, dramatic story that is both true and the Truth.

Even the life of Ahmad of Qadian, as preserved by the Movement, has been recreated as a series of stylized episodes in which prophetic justice is realized and an inevitable career is exhibited. There is, as far as I know, no canonical version of that history, but in a mythic mode it can be seen in several publications in English. In an eleven page "capsule," the (hi)story of Ahmad can be read in the Introduction to *The Essence of Islam: Extracts from the Writings of the Promised Messiah*.[22] A more detailed, but no less specialized account of Ahmad's life is presented in the first nine chapters of *Ahmadiyyat, The Renaissance of Islam*.[23] This narrative concludes:

> [Ahmad's] death was a grievous loss not only for Islam and the Muslims, but for the entire world of religion. He had demonstrated effectively that faith could be a living reality, governing, guiding and enriching human life, and not merely an academic verbal affirmation. His devotion to the Holy Prophet, peace be on him, and his love, admiration and appreciation of the limitless ocean of verities comprehended within the Holy Qur'an could not be exceeded.[24]

In the final chapters of that book, the "specialized" version of the Movements' history is told through the mid-70's. The polemical character of the history, an effect of the mythical mode of its representation by the author, is clear in the dramatic coda:

Religion and Mythology

> [Orthodox Muslim divines] fail to recognize that the only way of deliverance is through the re-establishment of man's relationship with God. In today's world the only claimant of such a possibility is the Ahmadiyya Movement. It not only puts forward such a claim, it furnishes practical illustrations of the truth of the claim.[25]

As in the Mormon case, the certainties that reverberate in these (artificial) histories are dependent on the convictional assumption that for mortals to know the Truth or truths a veil has to be drawn back. What Ahmad "saw" was that in his own person the power of the prophets of the past was revealed to the modern world. What we see is that a special history underlies the energy and the convictions of the Movement--a history specialized by being transposed into a mythic mode. And, again, history has become story, made out of dramatic episodes and infused with polemical and convictional motives.

These two sectarian examples allow us to see a singular process that is at work in all religious traditions. From both we have learned that history can be made out of unverifiable facts as well as out of facts that at least originate in the public domain. So far I have argued that the facts, whether imaginary or real, are **interpreted**; they are never presented without being embellished with meaning. Such facts never speak only for themselves, nor do they merely satisfy curiosity. The historical data are shaped under the influence of polemical and convictional motives, so that they are transposed into a mythic mode by an imagination that pries them loose from a particular time and place.

Special history is either revealed history or is the history of revelation. The revelation may arise from within as insight (as in early Buddhism) or may be objectively accomplished by an act of the deity (as in the three Semitic traditions). It may be expressed in realistic scenarios, as in the Baha'i Faith, or it may be cast as fantastic tales of supernatural powers and personalities, as in the *Rig Veda*. The sheer variety of mythic transpositions may obscure the consistency of the process throughout the world's religions, but it is clear that a special (hi)story is never missing from a tradition.

History Imagined as Truth

Before we push this judgment further, can we throw any more light on the process itself? Can we discover other ways to describe it that would give us more confidence in recognizing it when we see it? A special history usually presents us with a narrowly focused view of past events. Perhaps we expect a tradition's version of its own history to be one-sided and apologetic. But why should we expect this to be so, and how is it accomplished? An analogy may help us to understand the strategy and the motives of the selective exclusion that creates that special history.

Imagine a photographer whose trained and sensitive eye has just spied out what is to him a most beautiful and flawless blossom in a mixed bed of many different flowers. He wants to capture that blossom on his best color film in order to create a picture with aesthetic character. There are strategies for achieving that kind of composition.

Certain followers of a newly established religious movement are similar to the photographer in our analogy. They will be extremely enthusiastic about their founder or messiah, who, at least to them, appears as a beautiful or flawless person. When it is time to record the events surrounding the establishment of a tradition, the followers will want to present the "revelator" in such a way that others will be able to distinguish him/her from a multitude of other religious personalities as quite flawless. Our photographer uses the best film and a narrow focus that blurs out other items in the array. In very much the same way the devotees of a religious founder, looking back on past events, will record history in such a manner as to eliminate extraneous materials, events, or personalities.

Here I do not mean to imply any malicious plot to misrepresent historical facts. Rather, to return to the analogy, the photographer either cuts out or blurs the other flowers which to him are simply not important enough, or are too distracting to appear in the composition. In a similar manner, whether consciously or not, the devotees will simply not give much attention to extraneous personalities or events that are not essential to immortalize (or to mythologize) the founder. A special history, on analogy with a selective photograph, presents the founder or founding events from a particular angle and in a carefully arranged frame. In mythical history, we find selected out the special virtue and power that reside in persons and moments that stand outside of ordinary time.

The analogy demonstrates two basic points. First, a special history is a narrowly focused picture that selectively excludes certain aspects of a religious tradition's past. This story is influenced or biased by a group's unique enthusiasm for its founder or its faith. Second, unlike consensual and more objective accounts of historical events, the special history is used to convince the reader of the desirability, uniqueness and truth of a particular founder and the faith that he established.

Throughout our discussion so far, I have closely tied together the ideas of myth and special history. In fact, it seems to me quite appropriate to say simply that a special history is a species of myth, and a myth is an imaginative way of representing a certain range of human experience. Even in the most obvious fantasies there is some empirical content that has been transposed under the influence of intense conviction. The effect of such transposition is to remove what facts there are from critical scrutiny that might divest the events of revelatory power. To recast the information into an imaginative mode is to free it from its attachments to ordinary reality, to render it, quite precisely, extra-ordinary. A crucifixion, then, becomes more than an execution. The event is tuned to reverberate with a larger and grander music. The enlightenment of the Buddha under the Bo Tree or the vision of Baha'u'llah while imprisoned in Tehran point beyond themselves and become thematic moments in a great symphony. Such (hi)stories represent elementary historical moments as carriers of a mystery at last uncovered, of a truth that has been dormant and is now exposed. Those "priceless moments" are preserved under a full panoply of feelings and persuasions associated with them from the beginning, or at least in immediate retrospect. To transpose to a mythic mode, then, means to recreate an event or a personality as infinitely more than it could ever appear to be to ordinary discernment. A special history dramatizes what has happened or what has been, by refusing to delete from the account the feelings immediately and subsequently attached to the events.

The life of the Buddha is a good case in point. In order to appreciate the function of Gotama's "heroic biography" within the tradition, it is irrelevant to question the veracity of the special history in which that life is represented. The same judgment applies to the New

History Imagined as Truth

Testament story as well as to the portrait of Muhammad that emerges from the Hadiths. Ahmad, Baha'u'llah, Nichiren, Bodhidharma, Prabhupada, Confucius are all persons whose histories have been specialized and therefore imaginatively shaped in the service of Truth. A parallel judgment is that, even in the most fantastic myths, the ones about which we often say, "That is **only** a myth," there is at least some quasi-empirical content. Geographical, social, political realities are assimilated to imaginary scenarios in a grand mythological corpus. Fact and fantasy cross-fertilize each other in those (hi)stories that establish religious traditions.

Those familiar with the story of the Buddha will realize that it is not clearly fact or fiction. It is a species of history that serves the various needs of the community. The episodes are memorable because dramatically stylized. They individually and collectively carry the tradition's Truth and illustrate its teachings. From his unusual conception, through birth and itinerant career and enlightenment, to his entrance into paranibbana, Gotama the Buddha is the subject of a relentless drama, the problem of whose "historicity" is only a distraction to those whose lives are lived out under its influence.

The life of the Buddha represents the irresistible (but unattainable?) possibility of self-transcendence. That life also is a significant part of the special history of the tradition. It reveals an event of cosmic proportions, prepared for through past aeons and climaxing in a moment that has no permanent location in time or space. The enlightenment is an event that occurs in **a moment** outside of time to **a person** who is infinitely more than his human appearance. That moment and that person are memorialized in a story that comes to us thoroughly embedded in, but not contaminated by, "history." It is a history transposed into a mythic mode, esoteric, haunting, and quite literally an artifice, made by the imagination driven to articulate a vision of Truth beyond appearance.

In canonical and non-canonical renditions, painted onto temple walls, taught to young neophytes in pageant and recitation, unself-consciously preserved in the memories of the pious and the impious alike, the special history of the Buddhist tradition defies verification and refutation alike. The historical facts have been translated into dramatic fiction, the religious convictions have been represented in mythical

Religion and Mythology

portraits whose verisimilitude is captivating. The Buddha is the finest realization of that historical ferment in the sixth century BCE whose heady spiritual wine is till imbibed in the twentieth century. In the special history of the tradition, those historic "spirits" have been distilled and preserved ever since for the delectation of pious seekers. Transposing, distilling, dramatizing, photographing--whatever metaphor we choose for representing the process--the Buddhist traditions are grounded in the special history that memorializes a "priceless moment," the Enlightenment of Prince Siddartha Gotama.

Many other instances of special history could be cited. The Jewish and Christian traditions, of course, offer powerful temptations for analysis. Both possess a special history preserved in books that have exerted an incalculable influence on the Western world. An army of nineteenth and twentieth century scholars have tested the empirical content of those books. What they have discovered is that the theological motives have forced changes on the "facts." Beliefs and institutional interests may also account for the modifications of what consensus history presumes. Few have argued, however, that **imagination** is a sufficient cause for the historical transpositions that produced the two testaments of the Bible. Seldom, however, within the orbit of conventional analysis, have scholars explained the Jewish and Christian texts as exhibiting essentially the same process that produced the *Srimad Bhagavatam*, the traditions of the Prophet, the life of Baha'u'llah, the history of Adventism, or the rejuvenation of Nichiren Buddhism.

That imaginative process has produced some of the world's most compelling entertainments, histories that have held the attention of a full range of human beings in and out of season for centuries. There is no implication here that the special histories are idle or deceitful amusements. As "entertainments" they **lay hold of the mind**, providing existential distractions from the pains of life or powerful justifications for enduring those pains until they are alleviated. Patrick Burke has suggested that "the well-spring of religion is the experience that in some respects life is like a toothache."[26] I do not mean to suggest that mythic histories are like the "musak" played in dentist's offices to take the patient's mind off her discomfort. The entertainment value of traditional (hi)stories is more profound than that. But at

History Imagined as Truth

whatever depth of spirit they work, special histories do hold the mind, that is, they "entertain" the devotee.

What a special history most often holds the mind to is how some great personality has played a role in a drama that has redemptive power. Or it may recast events, real or imaginary, in such a way as to reveal unimaginable possibilities in the unrealized future. They may demonstrate the presence of a power that invades every present, or has mysteriously manipulated a particular past. But always, special histories show that more has gone on than has been dreamed of in the philosophies of mere chroniclers. They are windows that open onto a reality that only the initiated deserve to see, that only the willing can appreciate.

I have suggested that, as we wend our way into mythic traditions, searching out the characteristic behaviors and convictions that prevail there, we pay attention to the (hi)stories that are recited everywhere. Even if they are different in substance and detail, they are certainly similar in method. No coterie of the faithful can thrive without having created a species of history that preserves not only what may have happened, but what feelings and assurances are grafted onto the events. The fascinating thing to observe is what the human imagination has done with the facts and details, in order to convert events, real or imaginary, into powerful memories. Though one may eventually make some general statements about how and why such transpositions occur, the actual process that creates these epic scenarios can be seen in every enclave of a tradition. The special histories are everywhere available to satisfy the human hunger for the esoteric, to alleviate the pain that gnaws at the individual human soul, to provide a communal memory that hardly ever worries about verifiability. Our **approach**, then, is from the angle that allows us to recognize that in the territory where religious traditions proliferate, even history, both the events and the records of the past, are made to serve the Truth. Religion is that territory where relevant history, whether real or imaginary, is always specialized.

In practical terms that means that any special history is replete with judgments about the "intrinsic importance" of certain events or personalities. These are important first to the story teller and then, if his strategy is effective, they will be important to the audience. The point of view, deeply affected by a religious experience responsive in complex personal ways to some "priceless moments,"[27] will have biased the specialized account. In fact, this is precisely what the specialization of history consists in. Such (hi)story exhibits a bias, a slant, an angle of vision that discerns in or imputes to events a significance that may not be self-evident or self-explanatory.

A special history, then, is shaped by the intricate reciprocity of story-teller and audience, both drawn into a past where something inaccessible to empirical inquiry happened--or may seem to have happened. Eternity intersected time, a veil was drawn back to let us see beyond the limits of the mundane. A historic moment has become a window on the beyond and must be appropriately preserved in a special mythic recreation. Observing that process should allow one to find her way into the territory where people are being religious. The special history invites one to appropriate a past that promises to illuminate present and future experience. By becoming deeply familiar with a particular (hi)story, one's own experience is freed from a subjective labyrinth and brought into a new public, well illuminated, "straight" or "middle" Way. Along such roads, special (hi)stories serve the Truth.

Myths that have imagined the familiarities of experience are the entertainments that render dramatically the secrets of the world. We may, it seems, have come to a point in our history at which we prefer to penetrate the secrets of life in other ways. But as long as we continue to tell ourselves stories, as long as some among us continue to create fancies and fictions, as long as some among us continue to conjure dramatic renditions of experience--just so long shall the marriage of religion and myth haunt us.

From this point of view, religious experience does not so much depend on "believing" either the myths or the doctrinal formulas derived from them. Instead, it is in *anamnesis* that religious folks recreate the relationships that let them in on the secrets of the cosmos and of the inner landscape. This is a term, though found in the sectarian writings of Paul in the New Testament, points us to a general phenomenon in religious traditions. *Anamnesis* is a remembering in which one reenacts the scenarios captured in the mythic tales of a tradition. This kind of public ritual may happen in a movie theater or at an altar, in the singing of a hymn or in ceremonial reenactment. The venues are many

History Imagined as Truth

if not numberless. Perhaps *anamnesis* may even be the secret strategy in psychotherapy.

In the Eucharist, for example, the devout are instructed to "do this in remembrance." This is *anamnesis*, the reenacting of a mythic moment that actively recreates the event and makes the devotee a participant in the story of what once was. I am sure that many myths have been eroded over the decades and centuries and may have lost their power to engage or to enchant--much less to save. The annual ritual of enthronement that was the occasion for the recitation of the *Enuma Elish* has faded from use and from memory.[28] But the religious traditions of the world are replete with examples of *anamnesis* that are still viable and potent enough to hold together communities and even cultures. The mechanism of *anamnesis* is still in tact and focuses our fascination on the historical concatenation of mythological tales. And when such myths are married to religion, the two form a complex association that has controlled the human psyche and even history itself for millennia.

Notes

1 Will and Ariel Durant, *The Lessons of History* (New York: Simon and Schuster 1968), p. 14, emphasis mine.

2 Durant, p. 13.

3 Durant, p. 102.

4 *Ibid..*

5 Shoghi Effendi, *God Passes By* (Wilmette, Illinois: Baha'i Publishing Trust, 1970), p. xi.

6 William H. Walsh, *An Introduction to the Philosophy of History* (New York: Hutchinson's University Library, 1951), p. 66.

7 Walsh, p. 61.

Religion and Mythology

8 Thomas Patrick Burke, *The Fragile Universe* (New York: Barnes and Noble Books, 1979), p. 96.

9 Burke, p. 95.

10 I trust my reader will not consider this use of parentheses merely a cute trick. I mean to convey the judgment that a "myth" **is,** in every sense, a "story" and that "history" is also a "story." If a story is "the narrating or relating of an event or series of events, either true or fictitious," (See *The American Heritage Dictionary of the English Language*) the word may refer either to "history" or to "myth." The argument of this chapter is that what is "true" quite easily turns into "fictitious" narratives under the influence of the mythmaking imagination.

11 *A New Witness for Christ in America*, edited by J. Kirkham Salt Lake City: B.Y.U., 1960).

12 See *The Book of Mormon*, "The Testimony of Three Witnesses." (These witnesses were Oliver Cowdery, David Whitmer and Martin Harris).

13 James E. Talmage, *The Book of Mormon, Two Lectures* (Salt Lake City: Deseret News Press, n.d.), p. 26.

14 The history of Biblical criticism is well-known to some while remaining obscure to most. This, however, is not the occasion to review that history. Our agenda requires only that we realize that immense labor has been expended on testing the "historicity" of the Bible. That labor was undertaken with the greatest seriousness in the nineteenth century and continues virtually unabated today. *The Book of Mormon*, however, has not been subjected to such a barrage of "historical criticism." For this reason it is an appropriate example of "history in the service of Truth," created under the influence of that habit of mind that **imagines** those memories that may no longer be open to verification.

15 Peter Munz, *When the Golden Bough Breaks* (London and Boston: Routledge & K. Paul, 1973), p. 40.

16 Munz, p. 44.

History Imagined as Truth

17 *Ibid.*

18 The Ahmadiyya Movement in Islam has published many booklets putting forth its interpretation of the earliest history of Christianity. For example, *Deliverance from the Cross* by Zafrulla Khan (1978), *The Tomb of Jesus* by Sufi Mutiur Rahman Bengalee (1946), and several brochures. The Movement has also given credence to *A Man That Is Called Jesus* by A.R. Malabari (B. Khadija, 1981).

19 (The London Mosque, 1978), pp. VII-XVIII. The book was written in Urdu in 1899 under the title *Masih Hindustan mein.*

20 *Jesus in India,* p. 11.

21 *Ibid.*

22 Muhammad Zafrulla Khan, trans. (The London Mosque, 1979), pp. VII-XVIII.

23 Muhammad Zafrulla Khan, *The Renaissance of Islam* (Tabshir Publications, 1978).

24 Khan, p. 189.

25 Khan, p. 359.

26 Burke, p. 83.

27 I have used this expression several times throughout the essay. Though it does not appear to be a phrase of highly specialized meaning, my use of it depends on Malachi Martin's *The Encounter* (New York: Dell Publishing Co. 1971). In this book Martin tries to discover the "priceless moments" experienced by Moses, Jesus and Muhammad that established their respective traditions. It seemed to me also an expression that captures the quality of much of what finds it way into "special histories," that is, into the mythologies of any and all religious traditions.

28 I have read a manuscript by Dr. Harry Buck, Emeritus Professor of Religion at Wilson College, in which the mythic tale of Marduk and

Religion and Mythology

Tiamat (in the *Enuma Elish*) is interpreted as the paradigm of a struggle that continues to haunt Western Civilization. The *Enuma Elish* is the mythic hymn that, we suppose, was recited--reenacted--in the annual ceremony of enthronement. As such I cite it as a ancient example of *anamnesis*. Professor Buck sees the overpowering of Tiamat by Marduk as a public endorsement of "dominating power" as a political strategy directed against the "sustaining strength" of "she who gave birth to them all." (Surely one may see this story as a prime example of that seemingly unresolvable struggle between earth and sky, between male and female, and among all other natural and historical phenomena the "duality" represents.)The ancient Babylonian myth, then, continues to be **reenacted** on the stage of history, in rituals of war and politics, by governments and their elite minions who abuse nature and their own people. Historic myths and mythical histories never quite die, even though they always seem to be fading away.

CHAPTER II

MYTHOLOGIES AS ALTERNATIVE VISIONS

Imagine walking into a room where two three-year olds have been playing quietly (secretly) for over an hour. After a very quick survey of the room, you hear yourself blurt out, "What's going on here?" Now sharpen the focus of this imaginary event. You can shift the emphasis to any word in the question and express four distinct variations on your worry. Or you could add to the question the definitive adverb, and raise your voice in near panic: "What's **really** going on here?" The question, in this form, is the "open sesame" not only onto what a couple of three-year olds have been doing while you where elsewhere, but onto the universe itself.

"What's **really** going on here?" entails a confession. You cannot believe, in the first instance, that what you "see" (what "meets the eye") is all there is. The children have created a veritable chaos while involved in "happy play." They certainly did not **mean** to do anything "wrong" while they were enjoying their subjective but collegial reveries. So, to ask "What's **really** going on here?" is to confess that you are apprehensive, on the way to being hysterical, as you consider probing beyond appearances. And then, of course, there are the **motives** of the two: Was the chaos produced by two diabolic innocents part of a conspiracy whose psychic dimensions may eventually require the collaboration of a psychiatrist and an exorcist to unravel? Or was this all simply the accident of fun? How can you know "what's really going on" anywhere, for that matter?

Now imagine your question applied to a scenario of corporate mergers or to a series of foreign policy decisions. Or more mundanely, you notice holes appearing in your lawn without an observable agent. Your mother-in-law (or your boss) turns cold toward you, answering your honest questions with only a distracted nod or an averted glance. It may be that unfamiliar winged insects have begun to swarm near your basement window, or the well water is frequently muddy, or your youngest child stops calling home. Mount St. Helens has erupted after long years of quiescence; vast areas of beach have eroded under the impact of uncustomary storms. Two poets with wide reputations have committed suicide within two months of each other, and three youths within a ten block area also have taken their own lives with no notes to justify the aberrant behavior. Or perhaps eclipses of the sun and moon have occurred on two successive days or you have begun to experience a recurrent anxiety that is uncharacteristic for your normally sanguine personality. "What's **really** going on here?" More than meets the eye? Is there a pattern underlying such anomalous events? Or can you maintain the conviction, despite appearances, that there are no authentic anomalies? There are only events, occurrences, not independent, mysterious scenarios driven either by unknown or by sinister causes.

Can you read statistical charts and skewed curves without suspecting that the ozone is about to vanish or the ocean about to boil or the Boy Scouts about to pull off a *coup d'etat* in Omaha? Do we know what's really going on over the short or over the long run at the foundations of our houses or among our children, in the neighborhood or in the nation or throughout the world? And the solar system and the galaxy--are there protracted processes that slowly are shaping our personal destiny or the history of nature within that vast array of stars? Is there another ice age in the making? Will I be eligible for heaven by the time I die? Is there "anything" at all beyond death that should preoccupy me? Does that slight grinding sound in the right front of my 1982 automobile portend a major repair bill, or the irretrievable demise of the family car--and our having to go to the bank **again** just after we have consolidated educational debts of well over $50,000?

"What's really going on here?" is no casual question. Often rattling around beneath its elementary syntax are hopes and apprehensions, suspicions or fears that may be vague and unfocused. But always the mind longs for a pattern, minute or grand. What's really **really** going on may be trivial or momentous or even monstrous--once it is discovered. Life may be on the verge of shattering or may only be following a "normal" course. Rippling through phenomena there may be a whispered hint that "things are not what they seem." There may (or may not) be a process or pattern or a hidden agenda that is transpiring beyond our ken.

Mythologies as Alternative Visions

Religious traditions, each in their own way, will let you in on the presumptive secret of life in the universe. Each will tell you "what's **really** going on," even if you do not harbor any suspicions that "there is more in heaven and earth than is dreamed of in your philosophy." Hamlet knew that Elsinor was a stage for a moral and political drama that was inseparable from the ineluctable processes of the cosmos itself. Mormons have the same conviction, though many of them may not be able to muster the courage to discern the drama in all of its revelational detail. Buddhists and Taoists, Lutherans and Baha'is, Muslims and animists--all authentically religious people live with the hope, perhaps bred out of desperation or an inchoate fear, that "something else" is **really** going on than meets the eye. Ernest Becker said, "there may be an entirely different drama going on in this world than the one you think you see." The Buddha believed so, as did Jesus, Muhammad and Krsna--as well as Jim Jones, David Koresh, Marshall Applewhite, and the elite coterie of spiritual heroes who have focused the convictions and pieties of religious persons throughout history. The results may have been evil, as in the case of Jim Jones, the psychotic visionary who preached "revolutionary suicide"; or they may have created, as in the case of Islam, a vast historic community bound together by hopes of life everlasting. The practical consequences may have varied, but the determinant is always the same. A certain knowledge has been revealed or discerned that opens a window on reality that is otherwise closed to the unenlightened or to the uncommitted.

The interpretive idea that is emerging here may seem to make religion an unexceptional feature on the human landscape. When we consider the variety of circumstances in which the question seems pertinent, we may have to reconsider both our judgment and our attitudes with regard to what constitutes the phenomenon of religion. If particular expressions of religious traditions are really practical answers to that matter-of-fact question with which we began, then this most pervasive and baffling of all modes of human behavior may not be so baffling after all.

By arguing this way, however, we may be leading ourselves into a trap. We may be forcing upon religious traditions an explanation that is quite antithetical to their own self-understanding. From what I shall call simply the view from the outside, religion is a human

Religion and Mythology

phenomenon. Perhaps we can understand it from there only by neglecting the view from inside which may or may not intend to be a response to the mysterious question, "What's going on?" Still, a religious tradition, from inside, is not built merely upon doctrines to be believed. The devotees know something the rest of us on the outside simply do not know. Such knowledge about life and history and the future is the result of a veil having been removed from the surface of phenomena. Someone was privileged to see through a glass that was no longer dark.

Even if our approach to religion is strictly from the outside, however, we eventually realize that, in one way or another, religion is a revelational phenomenon, both in particular and in general. Those who try to comprehend a tradition with reductive explanations can only do so if they deny its own self-understanding. The dilemma, however acute it appears to be, may have a resolution which, though not definitive, may nevertheless win some degree of sympathy on both sides of the fence.

Let us allow that there is a subjective certainty that prevails on the inside of religious traditions that is based on the conviction that a superordinate reality has revealed **itself** and has also taken back the veil on what's "really" going on in and beyond the world. We may think of such subjective certainty as an objective datum within the environment of particular religious traditions. From the outside, the actual content of that subjective certainty (Julian Hartt used to call it "certitude."[1]) may be unverifiable, since revelation as a source of *bona fide* information is not easily credited from the perspective of the outsider.

Here the notion of "vision" may provide a bridge over the chasm between the uncritical devotee and the curious, often hostile, on-looker. For persons whose life and gnosis are defined by a vision of "what's really going on," a critical perspective may at best appear as an obscurely stubborn insistence that the universe may not be an authentic home for human denizens. But no matter! The vision brings its own certainty--or certitude. The insider "sees," indeed has been "shown," the pattern, the process, the grounds of intelligibility that provides the reassurance that "the mystery," even if it prevails, has a solution. It is possible, even if only by "believing," to know "what's really going on."

Mythologies as Alternative Visions

But "believing" is not quite the right word.[2] In ordinary discourse we often express our comprehension by saying that we "see" what is meant when another has offered an explanation. I would argue that this cliche is intuitively accurate, especially when we consider its use in discourse about religion. Persons caught up in particular traditions can legitimately claim to "see" the truth. First, of course, they hear what they "see"; but, once deeply accommodated within a tradition, they begin to "see" what they believe. How does such religious cognition work?

What a person **hears** inside a religious tradition is a story. The term "myth" is a quite convenient designation of such traditional stories as are recited and alluded to within the psychic and social boundaries of religious traditions. We have written about myth in other chapters, of course, but we shall be satisfied in the present context to delimit the term as an "imaginal representation of experience." Mythologies are not failed explanations of a reality that is presumably accessible to observation. Rather, they constitute what I would call a composite dramatic envisioning of **experienced** reality. By hearing such traditional artifacts, a person comes to "see" and to feel a certain version of "what's really going on." Before falling for the myth, a person's ordinary cognition gives only a working knowledge of immediate reality. Once the mythic version of reality has begun to operate, a different perspective is found. From that perspective, one may be overwhelmed ("convicted"[3]) by the knowledge of what previously had been obscured by ordinary seeing. By going along with the imaginal scenarios, by **hearing** the dramatic composite elaborated and exploited by priests, poets and shamans, one at last "sees" what has been "concealed." Such "seeing" is believing, and such "believing" leads to the conviction that one knows what's really going on.

The Greeks, for example, knew that nature could be grasped on analogy with a complex and cantankerous family. Their myths, at least as canonized by Hesiod and Homer, form a composite drama of a vast family of gods whose strategies and conflicts overlay the order of nature with a "transparency" through which one may see the otherwise obscure truth of things. The agenda hidden in nature is the resolution of dynastic conflicts stretching over three and more generations. The "immortality" of the parties to this conflict implies, of course, that there is no ultimate climax of that drama that is hidden before our very eyes. No one dies into complete oblivion, but the power differentials that set off the family quarrels continue within the very structure of the "dynasty of nature." Storms and fertility, male and female, ocean and river, earth and sky--all such "binary oppositions" are laid bare in scenarios of resolution and continuance. To hear of the unrelenting, often conceited imbroglios of Zeus and Prometheus is to "see" that the realities are continuous with familiar realities and with the deep psychic realities of extraordinary mortals and ordinary immortals.

The mythology of the Greeks, then, in retrospect makes sense through all of its convoluted development. It has come to us as a dramatic composite of tales whose effect is to take the veil off of the world so as to show it to us as it "really" is. The least and most that any of us can do is to venerate those absurd giants who connive and frolic on the Olympus of the human imagination. We venerate them because we fear them and we fear them because we recognize in them the very dispositions we discern in and among ourselves.

Hesiod's Theogony is the family album of the Cosmos. We thumb through it, our attention held by the elements in the mythical composite. And when we have come to the last leaf we should have a sense of the fundamentally dramatic character of that cosmos whose inner structure and dynamic are revealed by what conceals them in an absurd, though intuitively sensible, story of what we were missing. Now, with the help of Hesiod and Homer, Aeschylus and Sophocles, we can believe what we have seen and see what we have heard in the recitation of the dramatic composite of what, with an often dismissive gesture, we have called "Greek Mythology."

I believe that a similar reading can be made of other mythologies as well. However, for those who are not familiar with the details of such traditions, to march through even a sample of those composites, would prove tedious indeed. In order to make the detailed case for an interpretation of mythologies ranging from the Australian Aborigines to the Japanese, from the Iroquois to the Finnish, from those of the Indian subcontinent to the Roman Catholic, one would have to know something of the history of various peoples and epochs. I chose the Greek for brief comment because of a general familiarity that many of us enjoy. Others, of course, are not less intrinsically interesting than

Mythologies as Alternative Visions

the classical for persons willing to study them in detail as well as in the appropriate context. I shall be satisfied, however, if the reader would understand the interpretive hypothesis being developed here well enough to test it on other mythologies.

The main point is to think of any traditional mythology as analogous to a family picture album. With proper narrative guidance, by the family's priest or priestess, the pieces of the collage eventually fall into place to form a composite of dramatic images in which there is repetition and recurrence. The same or similar characters come onto the stage to exhibit behaviors that alternate between being unique and typical.

In a family album also, there is often the confusion of a hypothetical chronology. The effect of a guided tour through the mythic time that pervades the composite is a sense of emerging drama that promises unclimactic climaxes and subliminal motifs that slowly infiltrate the consciousness, until the listening seer may begin to mumble, "O, yes, I'm beginning to realize what is really going on in this mythic collage." But one had best whisper that to oneself, lest he be asked to clarify the revelation--and find himself unable to articulate it even after having been drawn in through the rituals of familiarity.

The imaginal content of Greek mythology and other such entertainments is obvious enough. I call such mythologies "entertainments," not to belittle their status in the human community, but rather to try to indicate their best effects. We have come to think of "entertainment" as performances aimed at **distracting** our ordinary attention. The notion that entertainment is escapist is consistent with such an unfortunate notion. Presumably we go to the theater or read a novel or listen to music or meander in an art gallery in order to forget those mundane concerns that press on us from the "real world."

If we pay attention to the term, however, it may clarify our thinking to recognize religious mythologies as, in fact, "entertainments." The word itself suggests some object or action that actually "holds" the attention. For example, the effect of watching a drama is to focus the attention on the stage, where action and characters are framed. The mind should not wander, but rather be captured, indeed, under the best of circumstances, fascinated, by the events and relationships that unfold. When the curtain comes down (when the

Religion and Mythology

album is closed) we may have received an appreciative knowledge that is intuitive and is based on impressions left by the artifice that has **entertained** us, that is, has **held** our attention.

It may makes sense, then, to say that mythologies entertain us. They direct and hold our attention on revelatory characters and scenarios. They may open our minds onto configurations of reality that otherwise would elude us. The irony is that the very myths, which seem to obscure reality beneath absurd fancies, may in fact be the occasions of revelation. By drawing our attention into the implicit depths of fictive dramas, religious myths allow us to see the veil being taken off the face of things. Mythological scenes may be grotesque imitations of the familiar. Eventually, however, by gradual accommodation to the extraordinary, we come to believe what we see. The mythic vision takes its time in coming. Soon enough, however, when it is joined to some structure of authority, the dramatic composite may bring to a mind straining toward conviction a revelation of "what's really going on."

Even though mythologies function as revelatory entertainments, the actual content or substance of the vision, i.e., of "what is seen," may vary. One could, of course, argue that there is a singular effect of any and all mythologies: They unveil (i.e., re-veal) what they conceal. Still, the "what" that is revealed varies under the complex conditions of particular cultures in real historic time. For example, behind the polytheistic veil of the Greek mythology, conflict is seen pervading *physis* ("nature"). The resolution of the conflict depends on power that is essentially "political," though apparently physical, that is, natural. The Christian mythos is quite different; another drama is in progress than meets the ordinary eye.

From a Christian perspective the relationships that are internal to the cosmos are not strictly familial or conflictual. Because primitive Christianity is continuous with Hebraic monotheism, there is not a plurality of powers that operate behind the veil that is thrown over reality. The king-subject relationship is the paradigm. Siblings and cousins, aunts, uncles, nephews and nieces do not become players in a cosmic melodrama. Nor are the conflicts sustained through generations.

In the Christian cosmos, created by the singular power of a lone deity, there is only one fundamental relationship that sustains the parties to the conflict. That is the relationship of Adonai to his

Mythologies as Alternative Visions

children, stretching serially from Adam and Eve, through Abraham, Moses, and David to Jesus, the anointed. In sympathetic protest against the vagrant behavior that defined this historic relationship, Jesus reassured his followers that the parent was inclined to take the initiative. The only thing required of the faithful, apparently, was a willed trust that the power of the parent that had been exhibited in all of its grandeur in the creation was also redemptive in the present. Conflictual relations would be resolved (and individuals would be **saved** from the evil seductions of Satan) by the parental mercy. The good news that reverberates in the mythos is that the initiative of Adonai is not bogged down by the same inhibitions and perversions that control the behavior of the children. In this story it is not the power of a Zeus that is the basis for cosmic assurance, rather it is the love of Adonai that recreates the Garden of Eden and thereby gives hope and "health" (i.e., *salvus*) to those insensitive to the ancient covenant between God and his people.

The Biblical mythos, then, reveals a different reality from that of the classical mythology. In the Christian vision there is a mediator that is a character in the divine drama. Jesus is the elder brother of the other human children of the royal Monarch-Parent. By "participation" in the mythic life of Jesus, the entire family of God benefits from the divine initiative. The denizens of the created world become actors in a drama of salvation. If the earliest followers of Jesus had not imagined the real drama in which the entire family of the royal Parent were actors, however unwitting, then the veil would have remained over reality. There would have been no visionary penetration into "what's really going on" through historical time.

Such orthodox mythologies, however, are subject to modification. It is the opportunity of sects and cults to respond to the objective ambiguities of the canonical myths, to change the focal point of our seeing until the reality hidden in myth can at last be seen for what presumably it is. Joseph Smith, William Miller, Miki Nakayama, Nichiren Daishonin, Srila Prabhupada, Emanuel Swedenborg, Baha'u'llah, Hazrat Ahmad, Mary Baker Eddy, Rev. Sun Myung Moon, Ramakrishna, Bhodidharma, and how many others have altered the focus of the traditional vision. Someone is always ready to **reconsider** what has been known for decades and even centuries. Someone is always

Religion and Mythology

ready to leaf through the family album and declare that it is incomplete or that most folks have missed some important pages over the years. But in one way or another, some new scenes or characters will be intruded into the basic mythology until the "real meaning" of its real meaning at last becomes clear. The examples of this process are legion. As with any good entertainment, different audiences at different times will be susceptible to different "readings."

The very fact that the "entertainments" come to us as dramatic **composites** suggests that, even without supplementing the album with more recent "photos," unsuspected "truths" can be discovered in pieces of the album/story that simply had not been well noticed before. But our task here is not to discover how new traditions or variants on old ones can be established. That is indeed an honorable pursuit and one that needs to be undertaken by students of religion. The present argument has only to do with an explanation of religion and its traditional proliferation that sees the phenomenon in relation to a common-sense view of social history. For the moment, we need to test further the interpretive idea that has so far been developed.

In this process we shall, I hope, come to appreciate the paradox that may stand for all paradoxes: **What** is revealed is **that** there is a mystery. Religious persons begin with some sense of mystery (or the mysterious?). Within and through the dramatic composites the mystery is exposed and its content revealed. That is, the devoted come to know "what's really going on." Hence the "mystery" is solved and the truth is cast as a message, a Truth, a kerygma--indeed as "a revelation." Hence, a "believer" may come to realize only **that** there is (or was) a veil hiding the truth of what is really going on. All of the "final truths" add up to the certainty that the "final truth" is concealed in the very myths that reveal it.

What is revealed, then, is **that** there is a mystery. Still none of us can steal from another the subjective hope or an objective promise by the tradition that the mystery is solvable. No one can take from me, because no one gave to me, the intuitive certitude that I have acquired from the family album or from a particular mythology. My conviction, in both instances, is that I am in the presence of a dense and intricate portrait of reality. Essentially I am satisfied with the mystery concealed in the revelational medium, though I am more than aware that others

Mythologies as Alternative Visions

long for (and many will therefore find) a resolution of the mystery. They will come to believe in what is revealed--until, perhaps, another visionary or charlatan comes along to see something different in the composite.

All things considered, being religious in a particular way involves being let in on "secrets." Such "secrets," of course, are not necessarily esoteric (though they may be so represented[4]). We are talking here about "imagined knowledge" available only to those who have been drawn into a context of ritual and conviction that is sponsored by a specific tradition or established by an agent of some tradition, such as a shaman or a priest, who may have to improvise an interpretation of the tradition in a crisis. A shaman, for example, may help to alleviate the private distress of a woman caught up in the throes of giving birth by leading her to realize that her pain signals participation in a cosmic struggle of generation. If the woman feels her private contractions to be related to an objective titanic struggle that is transpiring on the larger stage of the great world, then she "knows" something others do not know. Her personal pain is redeemed (relieved) when she realizes that she is not alone or that **this** birth is not an isolated event and that her pains are not unique to her. She knows "what's really going on!"

This situation was compared by Mark Leone to the experience of Mormons "going through Temple work." Apparently in those great exclusive structures of the Church of the Latter-day Saints, individuals are quite dramatically made witnesses of and participants in scenarios that are symbolic of what is really going on in and beyond this world:

> Consider then what is going on for the Mormon in the Temple. He brings expectations of profound experience and sometimes specific problems to be solved. Narrated before him by supernatural personages is the whole of human history comprising the creation, fall and redemption of man. At one point there is actually verbal and physical contact with God himself and then God actually invites the purified to enter and experience heaven. Throughout the narrations people are listening to Adam, God the Father and Christ talk, not as read by a reader out of the Gospels, but by people playing the heavenly beings. And for additional emotional impact the audience overhears private, off-stage conversations between God, Christ, Peter and others making plans

to redeem man based on his worthy performance. If he believes what he is hearing, the Mormon is hearing a level of reality not present even in "Revelation."[5]

The secrets of the cosmos, even beyond those projected in the book of *Revelation* are revealed in these temple pageants that allow individual Mormons to be drawn into stories that are "transcendental and unempirical," but are still "the highest things a living Mormon can experience."

If our minds can grasp an anomaly such as "unempirical information," then we may allow that a Mormon takes a "general piece of information...from the Temple. This is the knowledge of his place as a specific individual in the endless family."[6] This resolution of the earthly conflict of the single person and the society is represented in the Mormon symbol of the beehive. As Leone observed, "The beehive expressed the relationship of the individual to the ordered whole: the individual can realize himself only through his place in the whole." This relationship is "far more emphatic, far more latent with atomism, and sponsoring far more independence and idiosyncracy than we usually see in Christian churches."[7] Hence the Mormon is in on a secret that symbol, ritual and doctrine all elaborate: He is **in** this world but not **of** it; his most vital connections are elsewhere and otherwise. Each Mormon, for purposes of "temple work," is given a secret name that identifies him to "the god-impersonator" in the sacred drama.

These explanations of Mormon religious life are laid out by Leone in an article that tries to make sense of the peculiarities of the Mormon "temples." These "modern" structures are in effect artifacts that allow outsiders to glimpse the coherence and completeness of a system that defines and supports persons caught between two worlds. Leone puts it this way:

> The order and certainty of the beehive are both emphasized and partially created by the (Washington) temple's location. To get to it one must use the Beltway and go through the traffic of one of the country's biggest, busiest, and most depersonalizing and frightening highways. One Mormon, no doubt speaking for many others, has commented on the "contrast between Washington traffic and the peace of the temple." It is "like going to Heaven and

Mythologies as Alternative Visions

coming back again." The order and certainty of the temple are highlighted by the experience on the highway where uncertainty, tension, the immediacy of possible disorder, and the nearly total lack of contact with, and concern for, fellow human beings are all bred. Consequently the temple is even more meaningful because it represents guaranteed surcease and because the Mormon can see a truth which frees him from the mad world he had just driven through and which must, in sending him back to that same world, leave him changed and stronger. It does this by showing the Mormon his individual place within life and beyond it, and does so by immersing him in disorder as he approached the building and by immersing him in order once he is in it.[8]

Hence "the temple guarantees order in history and reduces the future to a function of acts performed now."[9] And as denizens of those other worlds that are built at the crossroads of this world, Mormons are privy to secrets; they know what's going on behind the veil that separates the empirical world from the transcendental. In the final analysis, of course, there is no question about which is the "really" real world. At least there is no question for the authentic and committed Saints of the latter-days.

Religious movements, wherever one finds them on the spectrum of history, are, or certainly at one time were, at odds with the society that surrounded them. The deviance of prophet or guru, priest or disciple, messiah or sage is founded in what we might call an "alternative vision of reality." That is, the religious person has not only a peculiar perspective on reality, but for him or her reality is actually configured in a peculiar way. The Buddha, for instance, was able, with the third eye of wisdom, to penetrate the veil of *maya* and to "see" that being, though constituted as becoming, "in realty" contains the possibility of a perfectly stable quietude. In an essay, "Renunciation," Bhikkhu Bodhi opens up the issue with great simplicity:

> The Buddha often described his teaching as running counter to the way of the world, and perhaps nowhere does this characteristic show up more clearly than in stress on renunciation. The way of the world is the way of desire, and those who follow the way of the world flow with the current of desire, seeking satisfaction in the

pursuit of their wants, cravings, and imagined needs. The Buddha's message moves in exactly the opposite direction: it finds the key to freedom in the turning away from craving with its insatiable, insistent drive for gratification. Instead of being surrendered to, the pull and tug of craving are to be resisted, the very mainsprings of desire eventually to be abandoned. The reason desire is to be abandoned is not that it is morally evil; it only becomes immoral when it impels actions which violate the basic principles of ethics, such as killing, stealing, adultery, etc. The reason for renouncing desire is, rather, that desire is a root of suffering. Though it appears to lead to pleasure and enjoyment, when examined closeup it is found to eventuate in dissatisfactions, pain, and ultimately despair.[10]

Some follow in the footsteps of the Buddha because they themselves are captured by the stories of the Enlightened One's penetration of appearances. He has seen what drives the human engine away from its original or eventual bliss; he has proclaimed in formula and parable what is our rightful possibility in the "breathless" state, nibbana. The Dharma is not preserved as argument or analysis. It is integral with the "second look" of a great personality, whose vision of reality shows us how things really are. Others may act as though the human person is by its nature rightly driven by those desires that relate it to "the real world." But the Buddha's alternative vision penetrates that illusion and makes accessible to our hope and practice a more accurate (a "truer") knowledge of desirelessness as the precondition of emancipation and nibbana.

Even in unfamiliar traditions or movements one finds the same implication buried deep in the surrendered soul. Yoshitsugu Sawai, writing about a relatively small religious movement that was part of "the rush hour of the gods" in post-war Japan, exhibits a wonderful confidence in the revelation to the Foundress of Tenrikyo, Miki Nakayama. In an essay entitled "Tenrikyo Teaching: An Insider's View," Sawai, in tone as much as in substance, makes my point:

> To understand what Tenrikyo "Truth" (*shinjitsu*) is, on the basis of these teachings (in the sacred books), we must refer to the first words of God's revelation spoken by God the Parent through Miki

Mythologies as Alternative Visions

Nakayama. The words are addressed to Miki Nakayama's family and relatives.

> I am the Creator, the true and real God. I have a preordination for this Residence. At this time I have appeared in this world in person to save all of mankind.
> I ask you to let Me have your Miki as My living shrine.

"I" in the passage indicates God the Parent. He is the Creator of all beings as well as the true and real God who protects them by his providences. Without God the Parent, a human being can never exist; this world is the body of God.[11]

These statements are unencumbered by qualifications. Sawai does not say, "'I' in this passage, **we may assume for the sake of argument**, indicates God the Parent." The sentences are appropriately declarative; there is no "if" or "perhaps" or "let us suppose." Neither the deity of scripture nor the devotee speaks conditionally. Revelation has rendered doubt unnecessary.

The notion of "belief" usually stands, in the conventions of religious discussion, for what I am here identifying as "a certain knowledge," a penetration, an unconcealing of "what's really going on." But Sawai is not talking about optional notions or subjective fantasies. Verifiability has given way to intelligibility in such discourse. We are here watching the emergence of a practical certitude that may be expressed in the imagery of a particular culture, or in the language of dream or myth, but the followers of Tenrikyo, whatever the medium of expression, **know** something that I do not know. In the *Truth of Creation* we learn that:

> Originally this world was an immense expanse of muddy waters. *Tsukihi*, God the Parent, found this chaotic condition unbearably tasteless, and thought of creating human beings so that He might share their joy by seeing their joyous lives.

The story carries us through a process of creation that to the uninitiated seems a hopeless jumble of quasi-natural characters. Eels and snakes and globefishes are transmuted into natural, bodily "functions." And at last "God began the creation of human beings, since the prototypes and the instruments had been decided upon." Then,

Religion and Mythology

God the Parent, reviewing the long history of human development, revealed that during the first period of nine hundred million and ninety thousand years, human beings lived in the muddy waters; that during the second period of six thousand years they received His training in mental power; while during the third period of three thousand nine hundred and ninety-nine years they received His instruction in reading and writing.[12]

Now we know how it was. Out of the primordial mud, God-the-Parent (*Tenri-o-no-mikoto*) created the living world and planned its human fulfillment. Even to the initiated in present-day Japan the story may appear as fantastic symbolization. But the truth about us and the Parent is clear. We now know what fundamental relationship prevails beyond the urban and industrial landscape; we know what constitutes reality, now at last unconcealed. Milan Kundera gives a handle on the truth that haunts the mythology of Tenrikyo or of any other tradition, for that matter. An artist in his novel, *The Unbearable Lightness of Being*, says about one of her experimental paintings: "On the surface, there was always an impeccably realistic world, but underneath, behind the back-drop's cracked canvas, lurked something different, something mysterious or abstract."[13] Mythical worlds are in their own, sometimes perverse ways, "impeccably realistic," at least on the surface. Kundera's artist, however, completes her thought with the paradox that justifies the religious person's trust in revelation: "On the surface, an intelligible lie; underneath, the unintelligible truth."[14]

Still, in a sense, the truth is intelligible, even if it is not susceptible to empirical verification. The truth of a religious tradition is more the truth of story than the truth of argument. The religious mind makes a synthesis of images in place of the scientist's analysis of data. In place of theories, the religious person has the insider's knowledge of the myth. In writing about the Bushman of the Kalahari, Laurens van der Post says:

> He knew intuitively that without a story one had no clan or family; without a story of one's own, no individual life; without a story of stories, no life-giving continuity with the beginning, and therefore no future.[15]

Mythologies as Alternative Visions

The knowledge of the story becomes in the context of a religious tradition an unveiling of true knowledge in the concealing allusions of the "intelligible lie."

We could, of course, go on, perhaps endlessly, with examples drawn from the extensive array of religious traditions--examples of the creedal claims and mythological scenarios that either contain or allude to what's really going on. Such knowledge is expressed in oracle and story, in historic formula and confessional utterance, in poetry, prose, ritual, and art. It is the cement that holds institutional structures together and it is the warp of a culture's fabric. The claims for such knowledge seem often the expression of delusional self-confidence. Sometimes the knowledge is based on unassailable but unverifiable claims of a direct revelation. And other times the knowledge of what is really going on seems to be the result of experienced insight or the visitation of angels.

The certainties of the first kind, it seems to me, can be found in "The Plain Truth: a magazine of understanding," the organ of Herbert W. Armstrong's Worldwide Church of God. The articles range over current events and trends with the promise of penetrating to the truth that is hidden behind appearances--as well as behind the daily headlines. The International Olympics, for example, are critiqued in order to conclude that:

> ...there is reason to believe that in the world tomorrow, after all the nations of this world have become subject to the kingdom of God--which will eliminate distrust and rivalry on the international level--there may be athletic spectaculars to far surpass anything this world has had to offer.

Another article tells "the untold story of D-Day" by offering "convincing evidence of the part a great unseen Hand has always played in history, and **especially** in the history of the Anglo-American people." We also find in the publication a reassurance that this Church has the clue to "...understanding the true nature of human nature." In other issues the ominous portents of volcanic eruptions, political failures, epidemics, embargoes, and the new sexuality are given a theological and biblical rationale.

Religion and Mythology

In an autobiographical essay that answers the question, "Where is the True Church?" H.W. Armstrong makes a characteristic statement that made his movement a strong example of the critical claim being laid out in this chapter:

> I had always believed in God--though I knew little about him, and just was not concerned about "religion." Of course, I had never researched the question deeply and thoroughly, to PROVE whether God exists, or whether evolution is true. Few ever have. I just took God for granted, and **supposed** evolution was a false theory. Nearly all who believe either in God or evolution have **assumed** their belief WITHOUT PROOF! But that was no longer good enough for ME! Now I had to KNOW!

The statement, in form and content, lets us know that H.W. Armstrong eventually came to know what is really going on.

The case of Emanuel Swedenborg is not so egocentric as this one, but it also is the story of a person who was brought to a plateau of certitude through direct revelation. The Church of the New Jerusalem, founded about 10 years after his death in 1772, offers its members a distinctive basis for a personal certitude. Swedenborg formulated his revelatory experience in the "doctrine of correspondence," a conceptual key to realizing the "marriage of heaven and earth." In effect, Swedenborg's visions have provided the decoding device for learning what's really going on in the Bible and within the natural and historical orders of reality. We shall let a classic text of the Church make the claim:

> The study of correspondences is of supreme importance, for as fast as we can learn to see in natural phenomena their spiritual cause and meaning we shall delight to turn to the parables of the Bible--for all its chapters are parable--and to read there, in this same language, of heaven and the Lord.
>
> Our guide and authority in the interpretation of the Word by the knowledge of correspondences is the revelation of its spiritual meaning given by the Lord through the writings of Emanuel Swedenborg. We find in these writings explicit instruction in regard to the spiritual meaning of certain books of the Word and of very many scattered passages, and a direct statement of the

Mythologies as Alternative Visions

correspondence of many objects which is a guide to the spiritual meaning of all passages of the Word where those objects are named.[16]

Then with a concluding denial "that correspondence is artificial (or) arbitrary," the author interprets "phenomena" as coded spiritual messages whose truth is "for our salvation."

Surely Muhammad, even if he did not "see" into reality, did hear recited to him what was written on the tablet in heaven. The Holy Qur'an, the record of that recitation, more than any other "sacred book," is "a word of several meanings." But the latent uncertainties are in the reader and not in the text. For the Qur'an is infallible revelation whose subject is Man: "It discusses those aspects of his life that lead either to his real success or failure."

> The CENTRAL THEME that runs throughout the Qur'an is the exposition of the Reality and the invitation to the Right Way based on it. It declares that Reality is the same that was revealed by Allah Himself to Adam at the time of his appointment as vice-regent, and to all the Messengers after him, and the Right Way is the same that was taught by all the Messengers. It also points out that all theories contradictory to this Reality, invented by people about God, the universe, Man and his relations with God and the rest of creation, are all wrong and that all the ways of life based on them are erroneous and lead to ruinous consequences.[17]

It was the angel Gabriel that wrapped the Prophet in a cloak and instructed him to recite these revelations.

The claims of Buddhists for Gotama are not as severe and categorical. His penetration came from the human side of the relationship to reality. He **saw into** the human person and found there an incessant changing of the components of existence that foreclosed on any sure knowledge of a self or soul. Upon "entering" nibbana one should realize the fundamental impermanence of existence. Gotama found that, in the human person, there was no Thing or Essence to be found. Beyond that experienced insight, however, enjoyed by the historic prince of the Shakyas, there have spun out myths and formulas and incantations that also function as the keys to true knowledge of the

Religion and Mythology

trans-human world. Jodo Shin Shu, for example, promotes "salvation by the Name--*Namu Amida Butsu*." In a wonderful inversion of the Christian notion of "the Word becoming flesh," in this late Mahayana tradition, the historic person has become the enchanted Name.

> The Name Amida Buddha was perfected as the "Dharma leading to salvation" and contains (embodies) all the virtues of having realized Oneness with Suchness, including the virtuous results of religious practices through long periods of time and the unlimited adornments and virtues of the Enlightened Buddha Amitabha.[18]

In Buddhism, then, the historical stream flows from humanistic insight to incantation. But the constant throughout all sea-changes of the Dharma has been the promise of true knowledge of what's going on. *"Amida Butsu"* may sound like a recognizable vocalization, but it really summons, in a way concealed from ordinary perception, the power of enlightened compassion that is the otherwise hidden substratum of reality.

Adherence to a religious tradition, then, pays off. The basic claims have gone through hundreds of permutations, but they always lead the convinced to the same certitude: "We know something that others do not know. We know what's really going on." One knows **and** feels that she belongs to the stars or that her redeemer lives. She may have the clue that breaks the code of history or that exposes the right path. But there is no religious tradition that does not know that it is possible to "unforget" our ignorance, to see at last what was veiled. Within every creed and myth and insight echoes the singular reassurance. Grant that there is an "unintelligible truth" concealed in the "intelligible lie," and if you will risk trusting that what conceals paradoxically reveals, then you have the basis of eventually knowing "what's really going on." We may choose the darkness or believe ourselves chosen by the darkness, but there is a light that either shines on reality or glows within it. By long practice or sudden illumination, some have discerned that light and in act and work have shown others how to unforget the self-imposed darkness. Such is the confidence that has empowered religious traditions from time immemorial--the confidence that their

Mythologies as Alternative Visions

mythologies contain and convey an alternative vision that reveals the Reality they conceal.

Notes

1 Lectures in Systemic Theology, Yale University Divinity School, 1952.

2 I have dealt with the problems posed by defining religion strictly in terms of the "belief paradigm" in Part I, Chapter II. Here the problem is more rhetorical than substantive.

3 A systematic analysis of the precise denotation and the various connotations of this term is developed by Willem F. Zuurdeeg in *An Analytical Philosophy of Religion* (New York: Abingdon Press, 1958). For example: "We take the term 'conviction' to mean all persuasions concerning the meaning of life; concerning good and bad; concerning gods and devils; concerning representations of the ideal man, the ideal state, the ideal society; concerning the meaning of history, of nature, and of the All. We propose *not* to use the term in any purely intellectual realm of discourse. We will therefore not say that a scientist *is convinced* that a certain hypothesis is true, but that he takes it to be true. We will say, however, that a Nazi was convinced that the Aryan race was called to lead the world." (p. 26)

4 As in the varieties of Gnosticism that can be found in the ancient world **and** in revivals in our own time, such as certain of the "New Age" movements. But the argument of this chapter is not "gnostic." The knowledge of what is really going on is not exclusively, or even in most instances, the kind of *gnosis* that one finds as the desideratum of esoteric traditions. Here the critical perspective includes such *gnosis*, but looks to understand any kind of presumptive "knowledge" that puts one in touch with the apparent mystery of things.

5 Mark P. Leone, "The New Mormon Temple in Washington, D.C.," *Historical Archaeology and the Importance of Material Things*, ed. Leland Ferguson (The Society for Historical Archaeology, 1977), p. 52.

6 Leone, p. 48.

Religion and Mythology

7   Leone, p. 47.

8   Leone, p. 48.

9   Leone, p. 47.

10 Bhikkhu Bodhi, "Renunciation," *The Washington Buddhist*, June, 1984, p. 3.

11 Yoshitsugu Sawai, "Tenrikyo Teaching: An Insider's View," *Bulletin: Center for the Study of World Religions*, Harvard University; Spring, 1982), p. 18.

12 See *Tenrikyo, Its History and Teachings*, ed. The Tenrikyo Overseas Mission Dept. (Tenrikyo Church Headquarters, 1966); Appendix, "The Story of Creation," p. 310.

13 Milan Kundera, *The Unbearable Lightness of Being*, translated from the Czech by Michael H. Hein (New York: Harper and Row, 1984), p. 63.

14 *Ibid*.

15 Laurens van der Post, *The Heart of the Hunter* (New York: Morrow, 1961), p. 171.

16 William L. Worcester, *The Language of Parable* (New York: Swedenborg Press, 1976; published originally in 1892), p. 14.

17 S. Maudoodi, *An Introduction to the Qur'an* (Lahore, Pakistan: Islamic Publications Ltd., n.d.), p. 6.

18 Seikan Fukuma, "Salvation by the Name--Namu Amida Butsu," trans. Shojo Oi, *The Pacific World, Journal of the Institute of Buddhist Studies*, (Spring, 1984), p. 17.

CHAPTER III

SURROGATE MYTHS

So far we have dealt with what I like to call "artifactual myths": stories of gods and heroes, of origins and endings, birth and death, conflicts and the resolutions of conflicts, stories of labyrinths and underworlds, of miracles and catastrophes--all cast as the tales of sibling rivalries and struggles with monsters, as tales of courage and cowardice, love and hate, power and weakness, marriage and murder, frustration and triumph, sacrifice and destiny. The variety of dramatic plots that have been dredged by the imagination and recreated in mythologies is relentless, but, one suspects, finite.

It is tempting, of course, to suppose that these kinds of artifactual stories are no longer viable or useful. We seem to have outgrown this way of seeing and talking about the world we live in. Some would prefer to dismiss them as quaint remembrances that are no longer relevant to our search for knowledge in the modern world.

But, it must be clear by now that we should not be so hasty. I am going to argue that even though traditional (i.e., artifactual) myths no longer seem to have much use--though even that is a doubtful judgment--we are still surrounded by what I shall call **surrogate myths**. This species of myth configures our communal reality as much as the old traditional myths did for the cultures of the ancient world and for the archaic worlds scattered across the continents of the globe. That is, I believe we are still imagining our world in ways that are quite comparable to the ways our ancestors did. We are still more dependent on mythmaking than most people suspect, despite a more apparent cultural preference for empirical accounts of how things are and how they should be.

In place of the traditional myths of the classical pantheon or the biblical story of creation; in place of the heroic tales of Theseus and Prometheus, of Rama and Krishna, of Jesus and the Buddha, of Zoroaster and Shiva, of Quetzocoatle and Vainomoenan--in place of

Religion and Mythology

these traditional myths, we have created for ourselves new surrogate myths.

We can discover substitute myths, our new imaginings, by checking out popular metaphors. A significant number now come from "the world of sports": end run, full court press, strike out, in the ball park, and on and on. There are, of course, other mythic worlds in which we find our figures of speech. We all have a repertoire of such figures that slip off our tongues with virtually no self-awareness. But those metaphors, those figures of speech that we use so casually are a clue to what I am calling surrogate myths. They are part of the cultural repertoire, expressed in the rhetorical gestures that allow us to keep our "knowledge" of certain commonalities accessible and useful.

Consider how much of what we think we know is really imagined! There are, I contend, vast stretches of our ordinary experience that we really imagine, rather than know in a strictly empirical way--that is, in a way that is rooted in "evidence." Let me get right to the point: Money, business, sports, sex, political power, automobiles, and celebrity are some of the content of our historical and communal reality. It is around these ideas--rather, images; or even better, "narrative images"--that our lives are, to some extent, organized. There are other centers, of course, but for the time being let these stand as the stuff of powerful surrogate myths that define our cultural milieu.

I do not really suppose that each and every one of us lives in a world that has **only** these images as exclusive centers. Our individual and social life is much more complex than that. We are not all robots programmed by bards and priests who exercise power over our minds and hearts. But whatever resistance any of us may muster does not obliterate these images that are always on the ready to shape our response to experience.

Here is an example: In virtually every historical culture one can find some kind of an Aphrodite. Who/what has become our surrogate Aphrodite? And in other civilizations quite unknown to us, we also find the images of sexuality--both male and female. An Aphrodite of our part of the twentieth century not too long ago published a book with the disclaimer at the beginning of the book:

Surrogate Myths

> Any similarity between characters and events depicted in this book and real persons and events is not only purely coincidental, it's ridiculous. Nothing in this book is true.

Well, of course, we have all learned that myths are not, in any ordinary sense of the word, "true." They are mere figments of the imagination--but figments, as we have argued, that become true in the telling of them. They are signs of our imagination trying desperately to gather together the loose ends of experience so that they fit together at least into a story that we can tell each other.

And Madonna (the name speaks for itself!) had been made into an image in which many of our fears and fantasies, our loathing and our fascinations, our dreams and our nightmares were brought into sharp focus: recreated as an image that the mind can carry around as easily as our wallets and pocketbooks carry our credit cards. And around that image of Madonna/ Aphrodite cluster stories, memorable scenes--the incidental dramas of daily life. If we are not still making myths, then how shall we explain the Madonna phenomenon? She is one of those powerful images in which sex is held at the center of our communal experience. One could venture to "deconstruct" that image, but for my purpose it is enough simply to identify it, to recognize it as a proto-narrative, waiting to be elaborated, waiting to be "applied" so as to gather the bits and pieces of personal/communal experience into a coherent, memorable story.[1]

What is the name of the baseball player in California somewhere who had signed a contract for 43 million dollars? That is a high price to pay for the convenient metaphors provided by baseball: in the ball park, out of the ball park, a home run, a curve ball, "Tinkers to Evers to Chance," grand slam, stolen base, king of swat, forced play, snag a fly, in the pocket, and so forth. But how do we really carry baseball around in our heads? As a drama, as a parade of heroes, as mental traces of sacred places: Camden Yard, Ebbits Field, Wrigley field, CandleStick Park, the "Diamond." Where is the Pantheon in which we have enshrined the gods and heroes of Baseball, with a capital B? In Rome or at Cooperstown, New York.[2]

And then there are the NFL, the NBA, the NHL, and Wimbledon and all the great skirmish fields where golf is played for fun and fame,

Religion and Mythology

for little wagers and massive prizes. And what about the quadrennial celebration of "pure sport"--before it became married to Business--the Olympics? How fascinating that this peak moment in international relations still bears the name of the sacred mountain of the Greek gods. My grandson who lives in Atlanta made a special phone call to me to let me in on his ecstasy when his city had lured the summer Olympics for 1996! A "religious" experience? If so, also, no doubt, a logistical nightmare!

Money and the automobile: What needs to be said? Isn't it obvious that the horse as mythical animal (whether with wings or with one horn, whether carrying heroes into glorious battle or racing across the desert, mounted by sword swinging Arabs with flowing robes) has given way to the automobile? The auto-icons sweep across our television screens, always exceeding the speed limit, always holding the road at wet sharp curves, always providing exquisite comfort in perpetual motion, always affordable--though, if the truth were told, the mechanical thoroughbreds can be bought only by the really wealthy among us. Even those, however, fascinate the poor and middle class for whom they are only a fantasy and the dream of a hope.

Lacking poets to conjure the epithets for the mythic machines, there is an enterprise devoted to naming the new gods that keep being born out of the heads and bowels of millionaire CEO's and the great factories of auto manufacturers? So we have *Infiniti, Lexus, Cougar, Ram, Celicia,* and so forth--names that become images that become enshrined in the pantheon of power where speed, convenience, mechanical beauty, and freedom reside as divine virtues.

And then there is War. Can we believe that only the Trojan War has been memorialized in myth? Think of the continuing evocation of the "Great Wars" on TV and in the movies. If we dredge our memories, I am sure that we will realize that the Civil War, WWI and WWII survive as mythical events. The Korean War, for us, is remembered in *MASH* and *Catch 22.* Is there any doubt that, to a large extent, "Vietnam" also survives as a myth?

It was Homer who celebrated the mythic war at Troy; now movies take the place of the epic poets. One need only name the films that have recreated the American "Trojan War": *Apocalypse Now, The Deer Hunter, Goodmorning Vietnam, Born On The Fourth Of July, Platoon,*

Surrogate Myths

Heaven and Earth., and on and on! That war haunts our imaginations not in memorable verses in ancient poetic meters; that war haunts our imaginations largely on the illuminated screen in the dark room. For a large portion of the population "Vietnam" is known primarily from the movies.

In 1991 an interesting book was published that attests to this fact: *Inventing Vietnam: The War in Film and Television*.[3] The Introduction concludes with the following statement:

> Each author invents Vietnam anew, discovers this or that meaning or significance while leaving open the possibility for other inventions, other discoveries. Vietnam, *as fact and as myth*, remains a central, contested area in American consciousness.[4]

But not only the historic wars are mythologized. "Desert Shield" came first, and then "Desert Storm," deriving powerful images from geography and weather in order to accommodate an entire nation to an episode of brutal mayhem. Ironically, of course, we were prepared for the battle by the mythologizing rhetoric of the President, who cast the situation in the middle east as a battle between good and evil, between Marduke and Tiamat, between JHWH and Satan.

How do we know the "history" of the western migration, from sea to shining sea, if not through the frontier myths of cowboys and Indians, evil outlaws and pure lawmen, able to draw a fabled six shooter faster than the speed of light? How have we understood the discovery of America, except through the heroic myths of Columbus. In 1992, there were no less than two movies and more than one television special that celebrated the mythical version of the Voyage of Voyages. Now, of course, there are some who have tried to turn the heroic myth inside out so that the voyage of discovery becomes the inauguration of the holocaust of the indigenous population of the Americas.[5]

If it were not for our innate cultural conservatism, it would be impossible to doubt that the movies have displaced the epic poets as the medium to which falls the task of creating and preserving mythical versions of war and much else of our near and far history. Our restless imaginations continue to revere the dramas that stir our patriotism or

Religion and Mythology

exacerbate our guilt. Both outcomes are reinforced by our mythmaking imagination.

Not only historic wars and invasions are mythologized, of course. The full array of historic vignettes that constitute a nation's past is recast from a variety of points of view, from the left, the right and the middle. We have all studied "American History"--or other national histories--in and out of school. Despite the sheer weight of the conventional stories, occasionally we are persuaded to attend to alternative versions of the national mythology; but that fact only underscores the prevalence of the consensus myths that have rendered archival memories as popular dramas and engaging images. Thomas Jefferson is one of the "Founding Fathers" for whom an alternative myth is being reconstructed by revisionist imaginations.[6] The comment of Jared Gardner in his review of *American Aurora : A Democratic-Republican Returns: The Suppressed History of Our Nation's Beginnings and the Heroic Newspaper That Tried to Report It* is telling in this regard:

> *American Aurora* . . . should be read by all who prize truth over myths, individual freedom over enforced national consensus, democracy over aristocracy. Some reader may be forced to surrender heroes or cherished myths, but all will find new heroes whose courage and convictions offer a more substantial foundation than the founding fictions. . .[7]

But whether we are fascinated by the conventional myths or by alternative versions, citizens have available a steady barrage of surrogate myths that capture a nation's historical memory. Without even realizing that we are getting wet, we all easily immerse ourselves in the stream of myths that feel like the truth that justifies one's loyalty or at least location in time and place.

And then there is food. Think of the relentless parade of icons that now are meant to seduce our appetites. The Hamburger has become a mythical presence on television and billboards. It is made to dance and sing, to lure us with its colorful beauty to gluttony and suicide by cholesterol. Tacos and piles of fried chicken, fiber-rich cereals and frosty bottles of beer and quasi-beer, steaks and lobster, french fries and garden

Surrogate Myths

salads: Images of a pan-mensal temptation of enormous (pro)portions. So even food, especially the fast kind, has been transformed through the ingenuity of the mythmaking imagination. That we call these inventions "ads" does not change the fact of their origination in that same fertile imagination that had earlier created what we recognize as myths.

How many other surrogate myths are there buzzing around our heads, telling us what is at the center of our communal reality? War, Sex, Fast Foods, Columbus, the Cowboy and "the West," Automobiles, Sports, the Machine, Money, the Past and even the Future--all these we will find hovering around the center of our national reality, enshrined there not only by our penchant for mythmaking but also by the power of the marketeers and political polemicists who now hold captive our once happy imaginations.

There is one more surrogate mythology, alluded to above, that is currently breaking into our communal consciousness, having been buried for nearly twenty years, though not obscured, since the mid Seventies. The original *Star Wars* trilogy is soon to be reissued in a digitally revised version--in preparation for the "prequels" that will be flashing onto the silver screen around the turn of the millennium. The difference between this "cinemyth" and artifactual myths, however, is its intentional contrivance. In fact, much of the mythology of the recent decades may bear such a mark, but *Star Wars* is an especially conspicuous example.

One of the engineer-artists who was deeply involved in this contrivance is Jack Sorensen, the president of LucasArts, the company that has grown around the *Star Wars* enterprise. He confessed that he was "as perplexed . . . as anyone" by the appeal of this cinematic extravaganza. He protests, however, that the creators of this sci-fi tradition had no cynical intention merely to fabricate and then to sell a new mythology.

> The demand is already out there, and we're just meeting it--it would exist without us. I don't know if I want to say this in print, but I feel like Star Wars is the mythology of a nonsectarian world. It describes how people want to live. People all view politics as

Religion and Mythology

corrupt . . . . And yet people are not cynical underneath--they want to believe in something pure, noble. That's Star Wars.[8]

The author of the *New Yorker* article himself comments on mythology in a somewhat critical mode:

> The purpose of a myth, after all, is to give people a structure for making sense of the world, and it happens that Lucas's heroic myths are an almost irresistible way of making sense of *him*.[9]

The italicized pronoun (*him*) refers to the creator of *Star Wars*, George Lucas, whom the author compares to Yoda, the superannuated Jedi Master who was the mentor of so many others who had mastered "The Force." So, this sci-fi mythology rebounds on its creator and somehow accounts for his charisma in matters aesthetic and cinematic. Such interpretive capability is part of the use to which a culture puts its myths. But even before the cinemyth began to interpret its own creator, Lucas had struck its roots in at least a popular version of mythology. In fact, according to Seabrook, Lucas "studied Joseph Campbell's book on mythology, among other sources, taking structural elements from many different myths and trying to combine them into one epic story."[10] *The Hero with a Thousand Faces* provided the paradigm for Luke Skywalker, the hero who "'beholds the face of the father, understands--and the two are atoned'." An extraordinary theological claim for a story that was conjured in its creator's mind "first as pictures, not as a narrative"! [11]

But Lucas himself was not completely naive or unaware of what his imagination was doing. He observed:

> "Myths, stories from other cultures. It seemed to me that there was no longer a lot of mythology in our society--the kind of stories we tell ourselves and our children, which is the way our heritage is passed down. Westerns used to provide that, but there weren't Westerns anymore. I wanted to find a new form. So I looked around, and tried to figure out where myth comes from. It comes from the borders of society, from out there, from places of mystery--the wide Sargasso Sear. And I thought, Space. Because back then space was a source of great mystery. So I thought, O.K.,

Surrogate Myths

let's see what we can do with all those elements. I put them all into a bag, along with a little bit of 'Flash Gordon' and a few other things, and out fell 'Star Wars.'"[12]

Out of this intuition, there has been worked into the culture a cinemyth that, according the Seabrook, lead Walter Cronkite to comment on the queues lining up for tickets, "'There's something extraordinary happening out there, and it's all the result of a new movie called "Star Wars."'"[13] Many have plumbed for an explanation for the tidal wave that has become a steady stream of causes and effects flowing through contemporary culture in the wake of this sci-fi trilogy--and its "prequels." Does this cinemyth validate the Campbellesque claim (ultimately derived from Carl Jung) that we all carry in our psyches and respond to archetypes that have somehow been realized on the screen? The question, of course, is rhetorical. What epics poets once did for us the movies now accomplish.

Star Wars quite literally **imagines** a future that feels like the past. It portrays, under an apparently mystical patina, the ordinary fascination with the human/cosmic conflict between "good and evil." We watch "ordinary human beings" struggling between the two aspects of "The Force" that, with a wonderful irony, preserves the integrity of the **human** person in a world populated by that strange array of benign and diabolical machines that threatens to displace the fragile creatures who created them.

The whole phenomenon of the *Star Wars* cinemyth may, from a skeptical point of view, be no more than a "tempest in a teapot." A myth so contrived, however "innocent" the intention of its creator, may in fact be no more than a distraction, unable to satisfy the presumably profound hopes and fears that were dramatized in more recognizable artifactual mythologies. Its promoters, overwhelmed and driven by their commercial lusts and fantasies, may have conjured only an ephemeral tale for the post-industrial minions; or the tale itself may overwhelm at least some of its audience with an allusive sense of profundity that may sustain them at least with a futuristic divertissement, while the real future lies hidden behind a mountain range of decades.

But maybe I have said enough. My point is simple--though perhaps a little confusing: Even though we might have outgrown the

Religion and Mythology

traditional myths--those ancient and seemingly irrelevant stories of gods and heroes--we have not ceased making myths. We have not lost the capacity to **imagine** the world we live in, of comprehending our experience if not always able to explain it, of grasping, of getting a hold of things by picturing and dramatizing what happens to us and what fascinates us.

So we continue to create myths that substitute for those that we seem to have lost or outgrown or discarded. These are what I have called surrogate myths. They often stand in place of the traditional ones--by now too numerous to catalogue. Those were the stories that used to define the reality at the center of a common life. The repertoire of such stories available in any culture may eventually become overwhelming in its variety and complexity. We are, it seems, tempted to think of those epics of heroes and gods as displaced now by "reality" as captured by journalists, historians and social critics.

I think what we have done, however, is to create substitutes for them--new and not so new surrogate myths: images of sex, money, power, conflict, technology, the past, the future, and so forth. These values at the center of our contemporary reality are **imagined** into heroes and new gods and amazing events that we have created out of the same mythmaking imagination that earlier created all the awesome fantasies whose presence glued life together for our ancestors. We continue to imitate those same ancestors in order to remember and comprehend our history and our desires, our hopes and our fears. We do this by appropriating those narrative images that transmogrify into surrogate myths "for our times."

Nothing changes--everything changes--nothing changes. And the wheel of history turns and within that great wheel our small wheels rotate, lubricated by the endless array of stories that we imagine out of our ordinary and extraordinary experiences. Our new pantheons, and the mythologies they inhabit, may (or may not) provide spiritual or moral reassurance. They do, however, bear witness to the penchant for imaginative conversion that sustains us as human beings who are contained within our private psyches, and at the same time embedded in finite communities and in an infinite universe.

Surrogate Myths

Notes

1. Depending on the decade in which one's personal memory is most at home, "Aphrodite" may have different names and faces. Madonna happened to be prominent on the cultural landscape at the time of this writing.

2. In mid August, 1995, of course, we witnessed the final canonization of one of Baseball's "immortals." He died of cancer after a debatable liver transplant that might have saved someone else less famous and affluent. Mantle was a "god" (hero) who became famous at least in part because he wanted to be a negative "role model." He sensed that he had been lionized (deified?) for his exploits on the "diamond" but also knew in his heart that he had his faults--in part given him by heredity, but also cultivated by himself out of a frustration and confusion too deep for him to grasp. So, Mickey (Mouse?) Mantle was a dual god: Herculean and tragic, a role model for all seasons and all types of people.

   And, then, there is the other (ambiguous) sports hero of the present-- the celebrity that we all own and who owns us, or at least our morbid attention. O.J. (Simpson) was raised onto a pedestal in the body social and then his "reality" was discovered by accident. Another "tragic hero," a demi-god whom we fear to emulate but whose presence has become impossible to ignore. I could go on.

3. Michael Anderegg, ed. , (Philadelphia: Temple University Press, 1991)

4. *Op. cit.,* p. 14.

5. See, for example, Kirkpatrick Sale's *The Conquest of Paradise* (New York: Alfred A. Knopf, 1990). One of the promotional notes for the book is worth citing: "It makes clear, in a fresh and highly readable way, how little we know about the man, and how much is myth. In a large sense, it seems to me to be a kind of myth-study; its the most illuminating book I've found about the great collision of Old and New World myths, with slices of raw reality sandwiched in between." (Larry McMurtry).

6. See, for recent examples, *American Sphinx: The Character of Thomas Jefferson* by Joseph J. Ellis (New York: Knopf, 1997) and *The Long Affair: Thomas Jefferson and the French Revolution, 1785-1800* by

Religion and Mythology

Conor Cruise O'Brien (Chicago: University of Chicago Press, 1996). Jefferson has also been re-mythologized in a recent film, *Jefferson in Paris*.

7 *The Nation*, 26 May 1997, p. 29.

8 John Seabrook, "Why Is The Force Still With Us?" *The New Yorker*, 6 January 1997. p 45.

9 *Op. Cit.,* p. 42.

10 *Op. Cit*, p. 46.

11 *Op. Cit*, p. 46.

12 *Op. Cit.*, p. 48

13 *Op. Cit.*, p. 49.

CHAPTER IV

MYTHOLOGY AND RELIGION
 :
PARTNERS IN A LANGUAGE GAME

A tentative application of Ludwig Wittgenstein's notion of "the language game."

So far we have tried to use the notion of a marriage as an organizing metaphor for our thoughts about religious experience and mythmaking. There are, of course, other ways to appreciate that venerable association. Ludwig Wittgenstein, with his notion of the "language-game" may offer a perspective from which to understand what has been going on over many centuries between these apparently strange "bedfellows."

Intellectual courtesy requires, of course, that we let Wittgenstein explain his own ideas, if we want to use them in trying to understand how Religion has managed to stay married to Mythology:

> But how many kinds of sentence are there? Say assertion, question, and command? - There are *countless* kinds: countless different kinds of use of what we call 'symbols', 'words', 'sentences'. And this multiplicity is not something fixed, given once for all; but new types of language, new language-games, as we may say, come into existence, and others become obsolete and get forgotten.
>
> Here the term 'language-*game*' is meant to bring into prominence the fact that the *speaking* of language is part of an activity, or of a form of life.
>
> Review the multiplicity of language-games in the following examples, and in others:
> Giving orders and obeying them -

Religion and Mythology

Describing the appearance of an object, or giving its measurements -
Constructing an object from a description (a drawing)-
Reporting an event -
Speculating about an event -
Forming and testing a hypothesis -
Presenting the results of an experiment in tables and diagrams-
Making up a story; and reading it -
Play-acting -
Singing catches -
Guessing riddles -
Making a joke; telling it -
Solving a problem in practical arithmetic -Translating from one language into another -
Asking, thanking, cursing, greeting, praying.[1]

. . . Here we come up against the great question that lies behind all these considerations. - For someone might object against me: 'You take the easy way out! You talk about all sorts of language-games, but have nowhere said what the essence of a language-game, and hence of language, is: what is common to all these activities, and what makes them into language or parts of language. . . .

And this is true. -Instead of producing something common to all that we call language, I am saying that these phenomena have no one thing in common which makes us use the same word for all, - but that they are *related* to one another in many different ways. And it is because of this relationship, or these relationships, that we call them all 'language'.[2]

Wittgenstein then goes onto explain what he calls "family resemblances" among various games, such as board-games, card-games, ball-games, and the like. The analogy, of course, extends to language-games. It seems sensible to me, then, that we might designate "mythmaking" and "religious experience" as language-games to be played out according to fairly well-defined rules. If that strategy holds, then we might seek such family resemblances between them that will allow us to appreciate how they diverge and how they "cooperate." So, instead of thinking of the relationship of Mythology and Religion only on analogy with a marriage contract as we have done up to this final

Partners in a Language Game

point, we might also follow Wittgenstein's suggestion and consider them both as language-games whose family resemblance may be like that of brother and sister or of grandparents and grandchildren. In the context of what has gone before, of course, the preferred family resemblance would be that of husband and wife--albeit "married of necessity."

Following our confrontation with Ludwig Wittgenstein, the following thoughts occur to me:

> If the application of the notion of "language game" to mythology and religion makes sense, then we are justified in asking two questions:
> A. What family resemblances exist between the mythmaking language game and the religious-experience language game?
> B. What are the rules of these two language games?

Let's address the second question first: One of the persistent rules of both games is "identity"; or, to put it differently: the non-distinction of subject and object. One consequence of this rule is the ease with which we attribute independent existence to persons and events that we have actually "imagined." Fiction is not necessarily distinguished from reality when we conjure persons from our memories or imaginations. It is this capacity for thinking in identities that Philip Wheelwright had in mind when he set out to understand "man's poetic envisionment of things." The thing and the metaphor can both be "imagined" as, in some sense, actually existing. Wheelwright's notion of *"the ontological status of radical metaphor"*[3] capture this possibility. Once we imagine "the gods" or conjure any event or entity in a mythical mode, we have established its virtual (real) existence in the very world in which the conjuring takes place.

Wheelwright objects that our current intellectual mores "restrict us, by and large, to the naturalistic point of view, allowing few or no beliefs save such as can be validated in the last resort by scientific method."[4] Hence we are not permitted "to envision--at least not with an equal degree of seriousness and public accountability--gods and demons, fairies and elves, or (in anything like a firm sense) inspiration

Religion and Mythology

by the Muses."[5] If we accept the confinement of our knowing efforts to such "mores," then are we not obliged to discard retroactively the entire corpus of mythology and its companion religion? Of course, we may keep these antiques in the museum of our consciousness, but dare we think that they are, in any sense, valid knowledge? Presumably, the sooner we free our minds of such distractions, the sooner we shall find truth valid for our location in historical time. Does such a decision, however, win a new freedom for us or capture us again in a universe that can tolerate only one way of being understood?

If we can learn to respect a variety of cognitive strategies, as I argued we should in an earlier part of this book, then a second rule of these games is the legitimacy of **imagining** as a kind of virtual knowledge. A third rule is the validity of **experience** in place of empirical knowledge as the basis of finding and defining ourselves in a world. A corollary of that rule is: Familiarity does **not** breed contempt but, rather, intuition and insight; it provides an experiential basis of naming and recognition.

Both games involve persons in *imagining* experience. They differ in the consequences of the virtual knowledge--that is, in the consequences of "knowing as," of celebrating the marriage in our thoughts of thing and metaphor, of perception and interpretation. There are certain behavioral consequences as we play the religious experience language-game: primarily, and in a most general sense, we practice ritual behaviors. On the other hand, the mythmaking language-game provides imaginary companions that help us account for what the world is and how it is.

The interaction of the two games may show itself in the following way: The mythmaking game provides the focus for (occasion for and justification of) ritual behavior. The religious experience game provokes us to *realize* [6] the imagined entities and events conjured in the mythmaking game. In the religious experience game, of course, revelation, **in some sense**, is operative in our finding a practical truth as well as a conviction of meaning or significance. But the fundamental rule that defines both games is simply that identity is the precondition of experience.[7] What else can be said about the **rules** of the two games? Both satisfy the longing for and the impulse to order and coherence. It seems as impossible for the mind to endure, much

Partners in a Language Game

less experience, absolute chaos as for a correlative reality to exhibit it. "Experience" is the "experience of"--what? Everything or Nothing? Are either of these possible as objects or occasions of experience? I doubt it.[8] In my best judgment, experience is usually focused; that is, the subject always has an object in relation to which it "defines" itself, though in the two games of religious experience and mythmaking, no radical distinction between the two is required for the game to be played. Or to put it differently: We are or become what we see, or we see what we are or may become.

In short, then, we may learn to think our way into religious mythologies by way of the simple realization that the human mind is quite capable of imagining persons and events and then allowing them to transform themselves into virtual ("real," "true") events and persons. The actual and the imagined, fact and fiction reflect each other as identities. The dramatic images, conjured by the imagination, take on a life of their own when we recite or celebrate the stories in which they are carried. Mythic tales are not so much told because they are true; they become true in the telling.

Such a notion, of course, implies that religious myths are fictions. As indeed they are; but it is quite easy to demonstrate a consistent, if not persistent, preference among human persons for fiction over fact. If, however, the analysis of mythmaking that has been developed in earlier chapters is at all persuasive, such a judgment does not mean that religious persons are habituated to lies and self-delusions. Infusing every myth is a content of experience that is quite recognizable. Some may be universally human, independent of time, place and culture; others may be such particular evocations of nature or history that our own imaginations may only be able to grope toward what is being imagined. Still, there are rules, knowledge of which may help us to "watch" (or even participate in[9]) the games being played with fair appreciation.

In this coda I have tried to suggest three such rules that apply to both the mythmaking and the religious experience language-games: the rule of identity, the legitimacy of *imagining* and the validity of *experience*. There may, of course, be others. But even though the rule book may be incomplete we may still recognize the general configuration of the two games and be able to discern at least a family resemblance. If the rhetorical figure that I began with holds any authority, then it is not too far fetched to see religion and mythology living at least as consorts if not under the strict contract of husband and wife. Still, I confess to a preference for the sense of intimacy carried in the critical notion of a marriage.

Even though some among us may think of marriage as a casual, occasional or even temporary association, Wittgenstein's perspective suggests the warning that the game that involves religious experience and mythmaking is not that way. And given the persistence of the complex relationship of religious experience and mythmaking, we should be more appreciative of the familial relationship of these two venerable phantoms that have haunted human societies from (near) the beginning.

Notes

1 To alert the reader to what lies ahead, I would add to this list the following "language-game": Creating (i.e., imagining) a myth out of the moments of religious experience.

2 *The Wittgenstein Reader*, ed. Anthony Kenny (London: Blackwell, Ltd., 1994), pp. 47-48.

3 *The Burning Fountain: A Study in the Language of Symbolism* (Bloomington: Indiana University Press, 1954), p. 97.

4 Wheelwright, p. 5

5 *Ibid.*

6 Here the term must be taken quite literally. To "real-ize" is to "make real," to imagine into existence. "Realization" bestows upon metaphors that are no longer **mere** figures of speech, "ontological status." (See Wheelwright.)

7 Perhaps we have here an explanation of our penchant for anthropomorphism: The world outside of our human heads is not "seen as" **other than** the world inside our human heads. After all, how can a

Partners in a Language Game

person know what she cannot see or see what she cannot know? And what do we always see and therefore know, when we give a look from within the labyrinth of our personal existence? Our human self or some semblance or aspect thereof!

8   Perhaps the exception to this general rule (that proves the rule) is found among Buddhist philosophers who seem able to collate Everything and Nothing in the baffling thought about "the Void" (*Sunya*). See T.R.V. Murti, *The Central Philosophy of Buddhism* (London: George Allen and Unwin, 1955), *passim*.

9   See above, the discussion of *anamnesis*.